I Prayed for You Today

365-day Devotional

Jane S. Joyce

Parson's Porch Books

www.parsonsporchbooks.com

I Prayed for You Today: 365-day Devotional

ISBN: Softcover 978-1-949888-74-4

Copyright © 2019 by Jane S. Joyce

All rights reserved. No part of this book may be reproduced or transmitted in any form or by any means, electronic or mechanical, including photocopying, recording, or by any information storage and retrieval system, without permission in writing from the publisher.

Scripture quotations take from AMPLIFIED BIBLE, copyright 1954, 1958, 1962, 1964, 1965, 1987 by The Lockman Foundation. All rights reserved. Used with permission. (www.lockman.org)

I Prayed for You Today

January 1

Today's passage describes the events of the eighth day of Jesus' life. We see the observance of tradition by His parents, the patience of a devoted servant, and the praise of a godly, elderly woman. Observance, patience, praise – all qualities to emulate in this New Year.

Luke 2:21-39

Jesus Presented at the Temple

21 At the end of eight days, when He was to be circumcised, He was named Jesus, the name given [to Him] by the angel [Gabriel] before He was conceived in the womb.

22 And when the time for their purification came [that is, the mother's purification and the baby's dedication] according to the Law of Moses, they brought Him up to Jerusalem to present Him to the Lord [set apart as the Firstborn] 23 (as it is written in the Law of the Lord, "Every firstborn male that opens the womb shall be called holy [set apart and dedicated] to the Lord)" 24 and [they came also] to offer a sacrifice according to what is said in the Law of the Lord [to be appropriate for a family of modest means], "a pair of turtledoves or two young pigeons."

25 Now there was a man in Jerusalem whose name was Simeon; and this man was righteous and devout [carefully observing the divine Law] and looking for the [a]Consolation of Israel; and the Holy Spirit was upon him. 26 It had been revealed to him by the Holy Spirit that he would not die before he had seen the Lord's Christ (the Messiah, the Anointed). 27 Prompted by the Spirit, he came into the temple [enclosure]; and when the parents brought in the child Jesus, [b]to do for Him the custom required by the Law, 28 Simeon took Him into his arms, and blessed and praised and thanked God, and said,

29 *"Now, Lord, You are releasing Your bond-servant to leave [this world] in peace According to Your word;*

30 *For my eyes have seen Your Salvation,*

31 *Which You have prepared in the presence of all peoples,*

32 *A Light for revelation to the Gentiles [to disclose what was previously unknown],*

And [to bring] the praise and honor and glory of Your people Israel."

33 And His [legal] father and His mother were amazed at what was said about Him. 34 Simeon blessed them and said to Mary His mother, "Listen carefully: this Child is appointed and destined for the fall and rise of many in Israel, and for [c]a sign that is to be opposed— 35 and a sword [of deep sorrow] will pierce through your own soul— so that the thoughts of many hearts may be revealed."

36 There was a prophetess, Anna, the daughter of Phanuel, of the tribe of Asher. She was very old and had lived with her husband for seven years after her marriage, 37 and then as a widow to the age of eighty-four. She did not leave the [area of the] temple but was serving and worshiping night and day with fastings and prayers. 38 She, too, came up at that very moment and began praising and giving thanks to God, and continued to speak of Him to all who were looking for the redemption and deliverance of Jerusalem.

Return to Nazareth

39 And when they had done everything [in connection with Jesus' birth] according to the Law of the Lord, they went back to Galilee, to their own city, Nazareth.

January 2

If you are called to a task by God, then perform it willingly and to the best of your ability. He will give you what is needed. Guard against using it for personal gain, which defeats the purpose to which you are called. To Him be all the glory.

1 Corinthians 9:16-18

16 For if I [merely] preach the gospel, I have nothing to boast about, for I am compelled [that is, absolutely obligated to do it]. Woe to me if I do not preach the good news [of salvation]! 17 For if I do this work [a]of my own free will, then I have a reward; but if it is not of my will [but by God's choosing], I have been entrusted with a [sacred] stewardship. 18 What then is my reward? [Just this:] that, when I preach the gospel, I may offer the gospel without charge [to everyone], so as not to take advantage of my rights [as a preacher and apostle] in [preaching] the gospel.

January 3

An amazing fact is, the more time we spend in prayer and reading Scripture, the hungrier we get for God. He truly becomes the one Being that nourishes our souls. Make time with God THE priority in your life this year.

Psalm 119:131

*131 I opened my mouth and panted [with anticipation],
Because I longed for Your commandment*

January 4

God is waiting for you. The Creator of all things is patiently waiting and longing for you. He wants to talk with His child and have that child talk with Him. Share your life with Him today. He's right beside you.

Isaiah 30:18

God Is Gracious and Just

18 Therefore the Lord waits [expectantly] and longs to be gracious to you, and therefore He waits on high to have compassion on you. [a]For the Lord is a God of justice; Blessed (happy, fortunate) are all those who long for Him [since He will never fail them].

January 5

Acknowledging God as our Master requires that we recognize all the roles He fills. He is not just our Father, but Judge, Ruler, and Ultimate Authority. Often, we just leave Him in one role, and appoint ourselves in the other roles. Take time to see if you allow Him to be your everything.

Isaiah 33:22

22 For the Lord is our Judge,
The Lord is our Ruler,
The Lord is our King;
He will save us.

January 6

Whatever trials you are facing, draw on Jesus for strength, and face those trials in His power. Through them, He will mold you into His image as He carries you through.

2 Corinthians 4:17

17 For our momentary, light distress [this passing trouble] is producing for us an eternal weight of glory [a fullness] beyond all measure [surpassing all comparisons, a transcendent splendor and an endless blessedness]!

January 7

Our Scripture gives the picture of a mother hen protecting her chicks. God spreads wings over us the same way. How wonderful to be cared for this way! Praise Him for His protection today!

Psalm 91:4

4 He will cover you and completely protect you with His pinions,
And under His wings you will find refuge;
His faithfulness is a shield and a wall.

January 8

Anxiety is widespread in our society today. As Jesus followers we need to remember that we are to cast our fears and cares on Him, not just once, but daily, minute by minute. Whatever the fears may be, even if we know we've caused our own problems, He still wants us to leave those burdens at His feet and cast our eyes upward.

Psalm 94:18-19

18 If I say, "My foot has slipped, "Your compassion and lovingkindness, O Lord, will hold me

19 When my anxious thoughts multiply within me, your comforts delight me.

January 9

God promises that new things are coming. That includes you! You don't have to stay caught in ways that hamper your walk with Him. God is able to do the ultimate makeover. Turn your concerns over to Him and see the changes that come!

Isaiah 42:9

9 "Indeed, the former things have come to pass,
Now I declare new things;
Before they spring forth, I proclaim them to you."

January 10

God can produce streams in the desert and throw mountains into the sea, so why would your problems be "too big" for Him? Don't struggle in your own power (which is inadequate at most). Give it all up to Him.

Isaiah 43:19

19 "Listen carefully, I am about to do a new thing,
Will you not be aware of it?
I will even put a road in the wilderness,
Rivers in the desert.

January 11

Did you know God has a tattoo? It's true; it is on the palm of His hand and it is your name. He loves you so much all He has to do is see your name and He smiles. Smile at your Father today and thank Him for His eternal love.

Isaiah 49:16

16 "Indeed, I have inscribed [a picture of] you on the [a]palms of My hands;

January 12

When you love the Lord, you delight in keeping His commandments and doing His will. The Christian life is not a dreary chore for you, but a blessing, a gift that your Father has given you through His Son. Praise Him, from whom all blessings flow!

Deuteronomy 30:16

16 in that I command you today to love the Lord your God, to walk [that is, to live each and every day] in His ways and to keep His commandments and His statutes and His judgments (precepts), so that you will live and multiply, and that the Lord your God will bless you in the land which you are entering to possess.

January 13

Unlike idle human chatter, God's Word is never without meaning, guidance, or truth, or all three together. The wisdom of this age will fade with the next generation, but the Word is timeless, reaching our hearts today, just as in centuries past. Be in the Word.

Isaiah 55:11

11 So will My word be which goes out of My mouth;
It will not return to Me void (useless, without result),
Without accomplishing what I desire,
And without succeeding in the matter for which I sent it.

January 14

God is faithful to destroy sin's strongholds over us, but, in addition, He casts our sins, great and small, into the ocean. We don't have to drag that ball and chain with us anymore. Free in Christ!

Micah 7:19

19 He shall again have compassion on us;
He will subdue and tread underfoot our wickedness [destroying sin's power]. Yes, you will cast all our sins
Into the depths of the sea.

January 15

God reigns from His throne, Creator and Ruler of all peoples and all the universe. Yet He leaves that throne if He hears His child's cry to comfort and to protect that child. You are that child. He is with you.

Isaiah 57:15

15 For the high and exalted One
He who inhabits eternity, whose name is Holy says this,
"I dwell on the high and holy place,
But also with the contrite and humble in spirit
In order to revive the spirit of the humble
And to revive the heart of the contrite [overcome with sorrow for sin].

January 16

Everything we have done and accomplished on this earth pales beside our bigger choice accepting Jesus as our Lord. We did not "do" anything. So, what we are proud of, and boast of, is what God has done and is doing for us. So much love showered on us!

Jeremiah 9:24

24 But let the one who boasts boast in this, that he understands and knows Me [and acknowledges Me and honors Me as God and recognizes without any doubt], that I am the Lord who practices lovingkindness, justice and righteousness on the earth, for in these things I delight," says the Lord.

January 17

Be careful in this day of false prophets who raise themselves above God, even while proclaiming they are His servants. God is everything; all glory and honor go to Him, none to us. Praise Him and ask for discernment in who you listen to.

Jeremiah 10:6

There is none like you, O Lord; You are great, and great is You mighty and powerful name.

January 18

We need never feel that we are standing alone. God is our foundation, our protection, our cover, our all. He is in front of us, beside us, over us, and behind us. We are His treasure, bought with His Son's blood. Feel his love today.

Psalm 71:3

3 Be to me a rock of refuge and a sheltering stronghold to which I may continually come; You have given the commandment to save me, For you are my rock and my fortress.

January 19

I often wonder how people cope with life if they don't have Christ in their life. In times of deeper sorrow and despair, we have the spirit who comforts, the Christ who loves unconditionally, and the God who has our names on His palms. Thank Him today for His eternal care and spend time with Him every day.

Psalm 34:18

18 The Lord is near to the heartbroken And He saves those who are crushed in spirit (contrite in heart, truly sorry for their sin).

January 20

When we work within God's plan and in His power, we can be assured of victory through Him. Not victory as the world defines, but everlasting triumph! Hallelujah!

Romans 8:37

37 Yet in all these things we are more than conquerors and gain an overwhelming victory through Him who loves us [so much that he died for us]

January 21

We know from scripture that the goodness of God is always present. Circumstances may momentarily blur our vision, but faith clears the view. Wait and see what the Lord will do.

Psalm 27:13-14

13 I would have despaired had I not believed that I would see the goodness of the Lord In the land of the living.
14 Wait for and confidently expect the Lord;
Be strong and let your heart take courage;
Yes, wait for and confidently expect the Lord.

January 22

We have teachers all through our lifetime, both good and bad. Our ultimate teacher is God, who guides us with His word and His spirit. Hold worldly teaching beside His teaching, to both judge and to decide if the instruction follows God. If not, discard it, and hold fast to God.

Isaiah 48:17

17 This is what the Lord, your Redeemer, the Holy One of Israel says, "I am the Lord your God, who teaches you to profit (benefit), Who leads you in the way that you should go."

January 23

We receive the anointing of God through His Spirit when we receive Christ as our savior. But that anointing is not stagnant. As we grow in the Lord, our purpose and knowledge in and of Him grows stronger. In truth, we are continually being molded and shaped. Don't rest on a one-time experience; seek more every day.

1 John 2:27

27 As for you, the anointing [the special gift, the preparation] which you received from Him remains [permanently] in you, and you have no need for anyone to teach you. But just as His anointing teaches you [giving you insight through the presence of the Holy Spirit] about all things, and is true and is not a lie, and just as His anointing has taught you, you must remain in Him [being rooted in Him, knit to Him].

January 24

Taking care of ourselves, eating right, exercising, and regular medical check-ups, is not vanity or self-centered. It is a responsibility we have to God honoring the "temple" in which His spirit dwells. With that realization, self-care becomes an act of worship and thanksgiving. Start your plan today.

1 Corinthians 6:19-20

19 Do you not know that your body is a temple of the Holy Spirit who is within you, whom you have [received as a gift] from God, and that you are not your own [property]

20 You were bought with a price [you were actually purchased with the precious blood of Jesus and made His own]. So then, honor and glorify God with your body.

January 25

Living in God's grace brings a constant flow of instruction, and gentle character-changing reformation. Our hearts and minds begin to desire that which God values, and we look further than this world to our eternal homes. Tap into this power source and be all that God desires for you.

Titus 2:11-12

11 For the [remarkable, undeserved] grace of God that brings salvation has appeared to all men.

12 It teaches us to reject ungodliness and worldly (immoral) desires, and to live sensible, upright, and godly lives [lives with a purpose that reflect spiritual maturity] in this present age.

January 26

A common misconception about the Christian life is that it is confining and involves a list of "do nots". If we truly love God, we obey because we love Him, and want to please Him. We realize true freedom is only attainable through listening and doing what the word says. Be free in Christ today.

John 14:15

15 "if you [really] love me, you will keep and obey My commandments".

January 27

This world may offer some comforts, but they pale beside being in the house of God. Nothing here will compare. Keep your eyes up!

Psalm 84:10

10 For a day in Your courts is better than a thousand [anywhere else]; I would rather stand [as a doorkeeper] at the threshold of the house of my God Than to live [at ease] in the tents of wickedness.

January 28

Do not fear man; fear God only. God holds your life in His hands, the life He gave you, and He will love you for eternity. Man can do nothing to you.

Deuteronomy 31:6

6 Be strong and courageous, do not be afraid or tremble in dread before them, for it is the Lord your God who goes with you. He will not Fail you or abandon you.

January 29

Praise to God is our created job. We were made for fellowship and praise. As you pray today, praise and thank Him for what He has done, and what He will do. He will answer your prayers according to His plan for you, and His answer will be perfect. Oh, what a loving Father we have!

Psalm 28:6-7

6 Blessed be the Lord, Because He had heard the voice of my supplication. 7 The Lord is my strength and my [impenetrable] shield; My heart trusts [with unwavering confidence] in Him, and I am helped; Therefore, my heart greatly rejoices, and with my song I shall thank Him and praise Him.

January 30

Stillness is a vital part of worship. In the quiet, we can hear God's still, small voice. We can sense His leading and feel the spirit's prompting. Be still today.

Psalm 46:10

10 "Be still and know (recognize, understand) that I am God. I will be exalted among the nations! I will be exalted in the earth.

January 31

God surrounds you with love and protection. He guards you as you accomplish the plan He has laid out for you. Don't be affected by others, either by their speech or their actions. God has you in the palm of His hand.

Psalm 27:1

1 The Lord is my light and my salvation—
Whom shall I fear?
The Lord is the refuge and fortress of my life—
Whom shall I dread?

February 1

We can live secure, blessed lives, knowing that God will never leave us. Even though we are flawed, and sinful, we can run to our father and He will never cease to forgive. He has an infinite capacity to love.

Romans 8:39

39 Nor height, nor depth, nor any other created thing, will be able to separate us from the [unlimited] love of God, which is in Christ Jesus our Lord.

February 2

In times of discouragement or worry, it becomes hard to see our way out of messes. Those are the most important times to reflect on the character of God, and what He has already done for us. When we rest our minds on Him, all other concerns fade.

Psalm 103:1-5

1 Bless and affectionately praise the Lord, O my soul,
And all that is [deep] within me, bless His holy name.
2 Bless and affectionately praise the Lord, O my soul,
And do not forget any of His benefits;
3 Who forgives all your sins,
Who heals all your diseases;
4 Who redeems your life from the pit,
Who crowns you [lavishly] with lovingkindness and tender mercy;
5 Who satisfies your years with good things,
So that your youth is renewed like the [soaring] eagle.

February 3

Our words can be the blessing someone needs so badly, or the hurt that wounds for years. Ask God to guard your lips, and heart where words originate. Encourage and love.

Psalm 141:3

*3 Set a guard, O Lord, Over my mouth;
Keep watch over the door of my lips [to keep me from speaking thoughtlessly].*

February 4

If you have doubts about ideas in teaching you hear, see how it holds up next to the truth of scripture. That is the true teacher for anyone on anything. Be on the watch for false prophets.

2 Corinthians 10:5

5 We are destroying sophisticated arguments and every exalted and proud thing that sets itself up against the [true] knowledge of God, and we are taking every thought and purpose captive to obedience of Christ.

February 5

As you scroll through TV channels, listen to the radio, relax with a magazine, or just sit thinking, ask yourself, "what would God think of this choice". We are to train our minds to prefer godly choices, just as we train our bodies to prefer healthy foods, and our children to make good choices. Pay attention to your thoughts for the next few days and see what you discover.

Philippians 4:8

8 Finally, believers, whatever is true, whatever is honorable and worthy of respect, whatever is right and confirmed by God's word, whatever is pure and wholesome, whatever is lovely and brings peace, whatever is admirable and of good repute; if there is any excellence, if there is anything worthy of praise, think continually on these things [center your mind on them, and implant then in your heart].

February 6

We often struggle with knowing what to say to people who are going through rough times, or those who have no knowledge of the beloved Savior. God has promised that through His scripture we will be equipped for all that comes our way. Relinquish your struggles to Him, and let scripture guide your words.

Isaiah 50:4-5

4 The Lord God has given Me [His Servant] the tongue of disciples [as One who is taught],

That I may know how to sustain the weary with a word.
He awakens Me morning by morning,
He awakens My ear to listen as a disciple [as One who is taught].
5 The Lord God has opened My ear,
And I have not been rebellious
Nor have I turned back.

February 7

Every trial, God loves and sustains us, even when we don't realize it until we have passed through the flames. Encourage others with how God has rescued and loved you. Never doubt His nearness.

2 Corinthians 1:3-4

3 Blessed [gratefully praised and adored] be the God and Father of our Lord Jesus Christ, the Father of mercies and the God of all Comfort,

4 Who comforts and encourages us in every trouble so the we will be able to comfort and encourage those who are in any kind of trouble, with the comfort with which we ourselves are comforted by God.

February 8

Faith is one of the essential building blocks of our Christian beliefs. Without a working faith, we only have head knowledge. Rely on God more and more for everyday needs, and not on yourself. Exercise your faith muscles.

Hebrews 11:1-3

1 Now faith is the assurance (title deed, confirmation) of things hoped for (divinely guaranteed), and the evidence of things not seen [the conviction of their reality—faith comprehends as fact what cannot be experienced by the physical senses].

2 For by this [kind of] faith the men of old gained [divine] approval.

3 By faith [that is, with an inherent trust and enduring confidence in the power, wisdom and goodness of God] we understand that the worlds (universe, ages) were framed and created [formed, put in order, and equipped for their intended purpose] by the word of God, so that what is seen was not made out of things which are visible.

February 9

As a nation we are obsessed with physical health. We visit doctors, consume vitamins, and make diet book authors rich. But… Spiritual health takes a back seat. Consult the Great Physician today and get a checkup on your spirit.

3 John 1:2

2 Beloved, I pray the in every way you may succeed and prosper and be in food health [physically], just as [I know] you soul prospers [spiritually].

February 10

A life lived in faith is God's richest blessing. A life lived in faith allows the freedom God intended, the freedom to rise above this earthly existence with its troubles, and keep our eyes focused on our Father and our eternal home.

Hebrews 11:1-2

1 Now faith is the assurance (title deed, confirmation) of things hoped for (divinely guaranteed), and the evidence of things not seen [the conviction of their reality—faith comprehends as fact what cannot be experienced by the physical senses]

2 For by this [kind of] faith the men of old gained [divine] approval.

February 11

God is with you always even when it feels like you will never get over the heartache or climb over the mountain in your path, the one you created. Trust Him and ask for His care, comfort, and guidance.

Psalm 34:18

18 The Lord is near to the heartbroken
And He saves those who are crushed in spirit (contrite in the heart, truly sorry for their sin).

February 12

The source of all knowledge and understanding is God. He has promised to show us great things. But, in order for that to happen, we must draw near to Him. Stay connected to Him through prayers and the word.

Jeremiah 33:3

3 `Call to ME and I will answer you and tell you [and even show you] great and mighty things, [things which have been confined and hidden], which you do not know and understand and cannot distinguish.'

February 13

Our souls' hunger for God. We can rest in Him, be strengthened through Him, and be certain that He orders our steps. What faith we can have through the knowledge!

Lamentations 3:24

24 "The Lord is my Portion and my inheritance," Says my soul; "Therefore, I have hope in Him and wait expectantly for him."

February 14

The Lord has good things planned for your life, but He knows you well enough not to give them all to you at once. Trust Him and wait for your gifts to appear in God's time.

Lamentations 3:25-26

25 The Lord id good to those who wait [confidently] for Him,
To those who seek Him [on the authority of God's word].
26 It is good that one wait quietly
For the salvation of the Lord.

February 15

In the book of Lamentations, Jeremiah was weeping over the nation's downfall. But even as he mourned, he still recognized the goodness and faithfulness of God. We can do that too, in the midst of our trials, calling out and praising the truth of God's unchanging character.

Lamentations 3:31-32

31 For the Lod will not reject forever,
32 For is He causes grief,
Then He will have compassion
According to His abundant lovingkindness and tender mercy.

February 16

We know that Jesus took our sins upon Himself at the cross, but we tend to forget that He pleads daily for us at the throne, He is our constant intercessor, our champion, even before we realized our sins. Praise Him today for His unwillingness to let us sink in sin.

Lamentations 3:57-58

57 You drew near on the day I called to You;
You said, "Do not fear."
58 O Lord, You have pleaded my soul's cause [You have guided my way and protected me];
You have rescued and redeemed my life.

February 17

God is with you. Do not fear. He tells us these two facts over and over, but just like the Israelites, we get lost in our minds. Take todays scripture to heart and deny your doubts. Trust Him.

Isaiah 43:1-3

1 But now, this is what the Lord, your Creator says, O Jacob,
And He who formed you, O Israel,
"Do not fear, for I have redeemed you [from captivity];
I have called you by name; you are Mine!
2 "When you pass through the waters, I will be with you;
And through the rivers, they will not overwhelm you.
When you walk through fire, you will not be scorched,

Nor will the flame burn you.
3 "For I am the Lord your God,
The Holy One of Israel, your Savior;
I have given Egypt [to the Babylonians] as your ransom,
Cush (ancient Ethiopia) and Seba [its province in exchange for you.

February 18

God's word never returns empty. He cannot lie and cannot promise what He won't deliver. He is the eternal firm foundation. Praise Him!

Isaiah 41:10

10 `Do not fear [anything], for I am with you;
Do not be afraid, for I am your God.
I will strengthen you, be assured I will help you;
I will certainly take hold of you with My righteous right hand [a hand of justice, of power, of victory, of salvation].'

February 19

The phrase "being a slave" carries negative connotations until Christ becomes your Master. Slavery to Him is a blessing, following Him is a joy, as day-by-day you become more and more conformed to His image. Accept His yoke willingly and feel the freedom of His love.

Romans 6:18

18 And having been set free from sin, you have become the slaves of righteousness [of conformity to God's will and purpose].

February 20

The quality of mindfulness is defined as being present in the moment. God actually commands us to practice that, being mindful of what we can do each day for Him. Stay here in the present and stay with God.

Ephesian 5:15-17

15 Therefore, see that you walk carefully [living life with honor, purpose, and courage; shunning those who tolerate and enable evil], not as the unwise, but as wise [sensible, intelligent, discerning people],

16 Making the very most of your time [on earth, recognizing and taking advantage of each opportunity and using it with wisdom and diligence], because the days are [filled with] evil.

17 Therefore, do not be foolish and thoughtless, but understand and grasp what the will of the lord is.

February 21

Through anything the world throws at you, hold your head up and remember you are a child of the King. He chose you and sees you as His own and His heir. The world will not understand the reason for your peace and hope, but you will as you hold fast to your Father's hand.

1 John 3:1

1 See what an incredible quality of love the Father has shown to us, that we would [be permitted to] be named and called and counted the children of God! And so, we are! For this reason, the world does not know us, because it did not know him.

February 22

In your own power, you will fail at being strong and courageous! But if you remember that the Lord, almighty and all powerful, stays with you in the path He has given you, you will find strength and courage beyond measure.

Deuteronomy 31:6

6 Be strong and courageous, do not be afraid or tremble in dread before them, for it is the Lord your God who does with you. He will not fail you or abandon you.

February 23

If God worked like the world does, we would suffer endless punishment and isolation for everything we've ever done wrong. But His grace and mercy are boundless; oh, how blessed to be children of God.

Lamentations 3:21-22

21 But this I call to mind,
Therefore, I have hope.
22 It is because of the Lord's loving kindnesses that we are not consumed, Because His [tender] compassions never fail.

February 24

God loves to give heavenly gifts to His children and waits for your request. Become like a child and ask your Father minute by minute for what He knows you need.

Luke 11:13

13 If you, then, being evil [that is sinful by nature], know how to give good gifts to your children, how much more will your heavenly Father give the Holy Spirit to those who ask and continue to ask Him!

February 25

Everything we could ever want, ever need, and ever desire, we find in Jesus Christ. Seek Him today, talk to Him, worship Him.

Zephaniah 3:17

17 "The Lord your God is in your midst,
A Warrior who saves.
He will rejoice over you with joy;
He will be quiet in His love [making no mention of your past sins],
He will rejoice over you with shouts of joy.

February 26

The key to a fulfilling prayer life is to immerse yourself in the word and in a relationship with the Lord. As much so that His will becomes your will, and your prayers conform to what He desires. Meditate on this and ask God to guide you.

John 15:7

7 If you reman in Me and My words remain in you [that is, if we are vitally united and May message lives in your heart], ask whatever you wish, and it will be done for you.

February 27

God's word never fails. It stands as true today as when first written, and as timely now as then. Never doubt that you can find your answers in the Bible. Spend time each day listening to its wisdom.

Psalm 119:160

160 The sum of your word is truth [the full meaning of all Your precepts],

And every one of Your righteous ordinances endures forever.

February 28

We were created to praise God. He alone is worthy of praise as Creator, Father, and Lord of all. Turn your mind to praise today, for what He has done, is doing, will do, and for who He is. Chase your dark thoughts away with praise.

Psalm 89:1

1 I will sing of the goodness and lovingkindness of the Lord forever; With my mouth I will make known Your faithfulness from generation to generation.

March 1

God is always with us, ready to comfort and encourage us when this life disappoints and hurts us. He welcomes us with open arms when we return from a prodigal journey, sorry for ever having strayed. His word speaks to us and never fails.

Psalm 34:18

18 The Lord is near to the heartbroken And He saves those who are crushed in spirit (contrite in heart, truly sorry for their sin).

March 2

The way to heaven is very clear; confess Jesus is Lord of your life, confess your sins, and confess you need His leading every day of your life. There are no surprises, no hidden requirements, no "gotchas". The Bible guides you.

Psalm 24:3-4

3 Who may ascend into the mountain of the Lord?
And who may stand in His holy place?
4 He who has clean hands and a pure heart,
Who has not lifted up his soul to what is false,
Nor has sword [oaths] deceitfully.

March 3

Whatever God assigns you to do, He will supply the power to accomplish it. Allow Him to use you; don't shy away thinking you're not enough. He loves to use His children to show His strength.

2 Corinthians 12:9

9 but He has said to me, "My grace is sufficient for you [My lovingkindness and My mercy are more than enough—always available—regardless of the situation]; for [My] power is being perfected [and is completed and shows itself most effectively] in [your] weakness." Therefore, I will all the more gladly boast in my weaknesses, so the power of Christ [may completely enfold me and] mat dwell in me.

March 4

We know, through the word, that we will have trials, which will shape and mold us in His image. Praising God during those trials focuses our eyes back on Him and off ourselves and reminds us where our strength comes from.

Hebrews 12:11-13

11 For the time being no discipline bring joys but seems sad and painful; yet to those who have been trained by it, afterwards it yields the peaceful fruit of righteousness [right standing with God and a lifestyle and attitude that seeks conformity to God's will and purpose].

12 So then, strengthen hands that are weak and knees that tremble.

13 Cut through and make smooth, straight paths for your feet [that are safe and go in the right direction], so that the leg which is lame may not be put out of joint, but rather may be healed.

March 5

King David knew that when convicted of his sin, he did not run away from God, but ran to Him and begged forgiveness. God gave him forgiveness just as He will us when we're broken by what we've done. Don't let anything stand between you and God.

Psalm 51:1-2

1 Have mercy on me, O God, According to Your lovingkindness; According to the greatness of Your compassion blot out my transgressions.
2 Wash me thoroughly from my wickedness and guilt And cleanse me from my sin.

March 6

God can speak a world into existence. He can breathe life into a man. He can level cities with fire. Trust Him with your life, your problems, and your love.

Psalm 98:1

*1 O sing to the Lord a new song,
For He has done marvelous and wonderful things;
His right hand and His holy arm have gained the victory for Him.*

March 7

Someday, God will come to judge the world. In His holiness, He cannot tolerate sin. Satan's rule of the world will come to a fiery end. But the children of God will feel His loving embrace as He gathers them to Him, and leads them to a new, celestial home. Praise Him for the forgiveness He has already shown you, and for the grace you will experience that day.

Psalm 98:9

9 Before the Lord, for He is coming to judge the earth; He will judge the world with righteousness and the people with fairness.

March 8

Spring is a wonderful affirmation of God's power in creation. Everywhere you look, flowers are blooming, trees are turning green, and the sky is bright blue. The birds welcome the season; the tiny hummingbird returns from winter vacation to delight in his antics. Praise God for blessing us with this beauty and look for Him in the renewal.

Psalm 75:1

9 Before the Lord, for He is coming to judge the earth;
He will judge the world with righteousness
And the people with fairness.

March 9

Your Father loves you more than anything. The same father has unbelievable power, the ability to speak a world into existence. Why do you think He has no power to help you? You have only to ask in His will.

Amos 4:13

13 For behold, He who forms the mountains and creates the wind
And declares to man what are His thoughts,
He who makes the dawn into darkness
And treads on the heights of the earth —
The Lord God of hosts is His name.

March 10

This scripture verse is so familiar, we know it by heart. But we often ignore the last phrase "as yourself". God intends for us to love ourselves, to take time for self-care, and to develop healthy self-esteem. Meditate on these words today and see if you are giving yourself some love.

Luke 10:27

27 And he replied, "You shall love the Lord you God with all you heart, and with all you soul, and with all your strength, and with all you mind; and your neighbor as yourself."

March 11

Many times we plan and execute only to fail because we are acting in our own power. Include God in your plans, even if you think it's too small to bother Him. He wants to be in your life all the time.

Hebrews 3:4

4 For every house is built by someone, but the builder of all things is God.

March 12

Today's scripture tells us to trust in and commit to the Lord, and also delight in the Lord. The first two commands often preoccupy our minds, but do we take time to delight in Him, much like a child delights in glimpses of their father? Look around and see what He has given you today to delight you and find joy in His presence.

Psalm 37:3-6

3 *Trust [rely on and have confidence] in the Lord and do good;*
Dwell in the land and feed [securely] on His faithfulness.
4 *Delight yourself in the Lord,*
And he will give you the desires and petitions of your heart.
5 *Commit your way to the Lord;*
Trust in Him also and He will do it.
6 *He will make your righteousness [your pursuit of right standing with God] like the light,*
And your judgement like [the shining of] the noonday [sun].

March 13

In America, we actively seek happiness, thinking it is our right and privilege. But God tells us just to seek Him, and then to seek His will. The Christian life does not guarantee happiness all the time, but peace that surpasses all understanding. Seek Him.

Proverbs 21:21

*21 He who earnestly seeks righteousness and loyalty
Finds life, righteousness, and honor.*

March 14

Nothing and no one can compare to our God. Look within yourself and make sure you are never placing on idol above God in your life. Give Him first place and glorify Him to the world.

Isaiah 45:5-6

*5 "I am the Lord, and there is no one else;
There is not God except Me.
I will embrace and arm you, though you have not known Me,
6 That people may know from the rising to the setting of the sun [the world over]
That there is not one except Me.
I am the Lord, and there is no other.*

March 15

God will always provide a way out, an escape, a rescue. Our part is to be attentive and prepared to obey. It may not be what we expected, or particularly wanted, but it is in His plan for us. Listen…

Psalm 18:1-2

1 "I love you [fervently and devotedly], O Lord, my strength."
2 The Lord is my rock, my fortress, and the one who rescues me;
My God, my rock and strength in whom I trust and take refuge;
My shield, and the horn of my salvation, my high tower – my stronghold.

March 16

Putting our faith in people, institutions, or politics is a dangerous and disappointing venture. The only place to put your faith and trust is at the feet of God. He never changes and never breaks His word.

2 Samuel 22:32

32 "For who is God, besides the Lord?
And who is a rock, besides our God?

March 17

The only concepts we have of God are based on our human interpretations. This limits our perception and essentially limits what we think God can do. There are no limits to God; accept that He cannot be defined and dare to hope beyond what you've ever asked before.

Exodus 15:11

11 "Who is like you among the gods, O Lord?
Who is like you, majestic in holiness,
Awesome in splendor, working wonders?

March 18

The foundation is the most important part of a building plan. If it is weak, the building will fall. Make sure your foundation is based on the solid rock, our God.

1 Samuel 2:2

2 "There is no one holy like the Lord,
There is no one besides You,
There is no Rock like our God.

March 19

God is not please with outward displays of "religiosity" before man. He is pleased with your love, devotion, and faith in Him, and your relationship with Him. Seek Him above all else.

Hosea 6:6

6 For I desire and delight in [steadfast] loyalty [faithfulness in the covenant relationship], rather than sacrifice,
And in the knowledge of God more than burnt offerings.

March 20

Everything we experience passes through the hands of God first. He desires our lives to glorify Him even when earthly trials happen. He is always our refuge and safe place and will stand us through it all. Praise Him in all things.

Psalm 91:9-10

9 Because you have made the Lord, [who is] my refuge,
Even the Most High, your dwelling place,
10 No evil will befall you,
Nor will any plague come near your tent.

March 21

The seeds we sow for God today may not come to fruition while we watch, but God asks that we sow, and He will water. Don't wait on the results but keep your eyes on God, looking first to the kingdom.

Hosea 10:12

12 Sow with a view to righteousness [that righteousness, like seed, may germinate]; Reap in accordance with mercy and lovingkindness.
Break up your uncultivated ground, for it is time to seek and search diligently for the Lord [and to long for His blessing] Until He comes to rain righteousness and His gift of salvation on you.

March 22

Praying for your city, state, and country is not only necessary, but God tells us to pray for our leaders, and to intercede that Satan will not have his way. Now more than ever, it is critical that we obey God in this matter.

Psalm 46:2-5

2 Therefore we will not fear, though the earth should change and though the mountains be shaken and slip into the heart of the seas,
3 Though its waters roar and foam, Though the mountains tremble at its roaring. Selah
4 There is a river whose streams make glad the city of God, The holy dwelling places of the Most High.
5 God is in the midst of her [His city], she will not be moved; God will help her when the morning dawns.

March 23

Jesus assured us that as His disciples we would have the ability to do wonderful acts in His name. But these acts will be in line with His plan and His will. We must continually submit to His authority and examine our motivations to make sure we are working for His glory.

John 14:12-14

12 I assure you and most solemnly to you, anyone who believes in Me [as Savior] will also do the things that I do; and he will do even greater things then these [in extent and outreach], because I am going to the Father. 13 And I will do whatever you ask in My name [as My representative], this I will do, so that the Father may be glorified and celebrated in the Son. 14 If you ask Me anything in My name [as My representative, I will do it.

March 24

How humbling to think, as Holy week begins, that the most precious gift we ever received was free! Our salvation was purchased for us at a dear price, by a Savior who suffered so we would not have to. Thank Him, praise Him, and daily be mindful of the events that took place this week, so many years ago.

Romans 6:23

23 For the wages of sin is death, but the free gift of God [that is, His remarkable, overwhelming gift of grace to believers] is eternal life in Christ Jesus our Lord.

March 25

People make gods out of many things: pleasure, possessions, teams, other people. But the living God, our God, never ends as earthly gods do. Worship the one true God.

Micah 4:5

5 For all the people [now] walk
Each in the name of his god [in a transient relationship]
As for us, we shall walk [securely]
In the name of the Lord our [true] God forever and ever.

March 26

Our walk with God should be simple, according to Micah. But, in our human way, we add and interpret, and come up with a list of things we have to do to satisfy Him. Take a good look at your life and go back to the basics of what God says.

Micah 6:8

8 He has told you, O man, what is good;
And what does the Lord require of you
Except to be just, and to love [and to diligently practice] kindness (compassion),
And to walk humbly with your God [Setting aside any overblown sense of importance or self-righteousness]?

March 27

Rushing ahead of God always ends in disaster. Remember Sarah's plan to get a child? The repercussions still exist today. Ask God for guidance, and then wait on His replay. Be patient and let it form according to His plan.

Micah 7:7

7 But as for me, I will look expectantly for the Lord and with confidence in Him I will keep watch; I will wait [with confident expectation] for the God of my salvation.
My God will hear me.

March 28

God knows you. You can never feel that no one understands you, because He does. He will never leave you or cease to call for you because you did something He did not like. His forgiveness is unending, and His love is eternal.

Nahum 1:7

7 The Lord is good
A strength and stronghold in the day of trouble;
He knows [He recognizes, cares for, and understands fully] those who take refuge and trust in Him.

March 29

God gave deer the special ability to climb in places that seem impossible. And He created our hearts with the ability to connect with Him in an even-higher knowledge and relationship. Let your heart climb toward Him, steady and sure, in the path He created for you.

Habakkuk 3:19

*19 The Lod God is my strength [my source of courage, my invincible army]; He has made my feet [steady and sure] like hinds' feet
And makes me walk [forward with spiritual confidence] on my high places [of challenge and responsibility].*

March 30

Today is Good Friday, Christ was crucified, and the temple vail was torn in two, allowing our access to God. Jesus took our sins upon Himself and gave us the ability to speak to God ourselves any time, any place, praise Him!

Zephaniah 3:17

*17 "The Lord your God is in your midst,
A Warrior who saves.
He will rejoice over you with joy;
He will be quiet in His love [making no mention of your past sins],
He will rejoice over you with shouts of joy.*

March 31

God's word is full of the promises He has given us, His truth. When we read and believe, we are confident that we can approach Him and ask that the promise we claim will be fulfilled. Seek your promises today.

Psalm 145:18

18 The Lord is near to all who call on Him,
To all who call on Him in truth (without guile).

April 1

It is hard to emulate Christ's example; in fact, it is a constant battle with our fleshy reactions. We want to do the opposite most times of what Jesus would do or how He would react. This is when we need His strength most. If He can conquer death, He can conquer our fleshy responses.

Zechariah 7:9

9 "Thus has the Lord of hosts said, `Dispense true justice and practice kindness and compassion, to each other;

April 2

Through God's grace, we receive salvation, direction, wisdom, and everlasting life and love. Grace is free, we do nothing to earn it, and though we are undeserving, grace is poured on us constantly. Accept grace and thank God for His compassion on us.

Titus 2:11-14

11 For the [remarkable, undeserved] grace of God that *brings salvation has appeared to all men. 12 It teaches us to reject ungodliness and worldly (immoral) desires, and to live sensible, upright, and godly lives [lives with a purpose that reflect spiritual maturity] in this present age, 13 awaiting and confidently expecting the [fulfillment of our] blessed hope and the glorious appearing of our great God and Savior, Christ Jesus, 14 who [willingly] gave Himself [to be crucified] on our behalf to redeem us and purchase our freedom from all wickedness, and to purify for Himself a chosen and very special people to be His possession, who are enthusiastic for doing what is good.*

April 3

You are a new creation in Christ. When the old habits and ways of thinking try to come back, remember you are brand new, and those things will only stain your shining countenance. Refute them with God's word and promises.

2 Corinthians 5:17

17 Therefore is anyone is in Christ [that is, grafted in, joined to Him by faith in Him as Savior], he is a new creature [reborn and renewed by the Holy Spirit]; the old things [the previous moral and spiritual condition] have passed away. Behold, new things have come [because spiritual awakening bring a new life].

April 4

When you are overwhelmed and feel powerless, remember those are the times God does His most powerful work. When you are weak, He is strong. Turn your thoughts to praising Him and wait on Him to show you what He can do.

Psalm 113:4-9

4 The Lord is high above all nations,
And His glory above the heavens.
5 Who is like the Lord our God,
Who is enthroned on high,
6 Who humbles Himself to regard
The heavens and the earth?
7 He raises the poor out of the dust
And lifts the needy from the ash heap,
8 That He may seat them with princes,
With the princes of His people.
9 He makes the barren women live in the house
As a joyful mother of children. Praise the Lord! (Hallelujah!)

April 5

God's grace never ends. When we confess a sin (or several sins) our relationship with Him is renewed, and we are again as white as snow. Let Him search your heart and reveal any stains you may need washed away.

Ezekiel 36:25-27

25 Then I will sprinkle clean water on you, and you will be clean; I will cleanse you from all your uncleanness and from all your idols. 26 Moreover, I will give you a new heart and put a new spirit within you, and I will remover the heart of stone from your flesh and give you a heart of flesh. 27 I will put my Spirit within you and cause you to walk in My statutes, and you will keep My ordinances and do them.

April 6

Jesus's sacrifice enabled you to have personal access to the God of the universe. You can talk to Him anytime, anyplace, out loud, inside your mind; complete and total access. Are you talking to Him? Open the lines of communication and keep it open.

2 Corinthians 5:21

21 He made Christ who knew no sin to [judicially] be sin on our behalf, so that in Him we would become the righteousness of God [that is, we would be made acceptable to Him and placed in a right relationship with Him by His gracious lovingkindness].

April 7

The way of Jesus is difficult for the world to understand. You have the key though, in the Holy Spirit who dwells within each believer. Be alert for the prompts and revelations the Spirit is eager to give you.

John 14:17

17 the Spirit of Truth, whom the world cannot receive [and take to its heart] because it does not see Him or know Him, but you know him because He (the Holy Spirit) remains with you continually and will be in you.

April 8

Never lose sight of the fact that God is the Ruler over heaven and earth. He will prevail. He deserves our praise for this fact alone. He is our father.

1 Chronicles 29:10-11

10 Therefore David blessed the Lord in the sight of all the assembly and said, "Blessed, praise, adored, and thanked are you, O Lord God of Israel (Jacob) our father, forever and ever.

11 Yours, O Lord, is the greatness and the power and the glory and the victory and the majesty, indeed everything that is in the heavens and on the earth; Yours is the dominion and kingdom, O Lord, and You exalt Yourself as head over all.

April 9

When we are totally sold out for Christ, we hunger for His word and His relationship, for His will. That brings true joy in the face of any obstacle that appears in our path. Care only for His opinion.

Jeremiah 29:13

13 The [with a deep longing] you will seek Me and require Me [as a vital necessity] and [you will] find Me when you search for Me with all your heart.

April 10

While God's requirements for us may seem simple, we cannot live them without staying in the Word and in constant prayer. We are powerless in our own strengths; He gives us what we need to persevere.

Micah 6:8

8 He has told you, O man, what is good;
And what does the Lord require of you
Except to be just, and to love [and to diligently practice] kindness (compassion),
And to walk humbly with your God [setting aside any overblown sense of importance or self-righteousness]?

April 11

Your life is meant to glorify God. That's why you entrust Him to guard your actions and speech. At no time, do you wish to dishonor Him or bring doubt to your testimony. Always let others see Him through you.

Psalm 115:1-2

1 Not to us, O Lord, not to us,
But to Your name give glory
Because of Your lovingkindness, because of Your truth
And faithfulness.
2 Why should the nations say,
"where, now, is their God?"

April 12

God's Word needs to be so precious to us that it becomes part of the fiber of our wings. It has to be the guiding force of our speech and actions, our "default", what we unconsciously revert to in times of crisis. Saturate your mind with the Word today.

Proverbs 3:1-4

1 My son, do not forget my teaching,
But let your heart keep my commandments;
2 For length of days and years of life [worth living]
And tranquility and prosperity [the wholeness of life's blessings] they will add to you.
3 Do not let mercy and kindness and truth leave you
[instead let these qualities define you];
Bind them [securely] around your neck,
Write them on the tablet of your heart.
4 So find favor and high esteem in the fight of God and man.

April 13

The Bible is miraculous; it not only reveals God's character and precepts to us, but it changes our hearts, making us each day a little more in the likeness of Him. Some books entertain, some are thought-provoking, but only the Bible communicates to us straight from God's heart to ours.

Psalm 119:11-12

11 Your word I have treasured and stored in my heart,
That I may not sin against You.
12 Blessed and reverently praised are You, O Lord;
Teach me Your statutes.

April 14

We are in God's presence constantly we are in His sight and mind at all times. If we would think about this fact more, maybe some of our choices would be different.

Genesis 17:1

1 When Abram was ninety-nine years old, the Lord appeared to him and said, "I am God Almighty; Walk [habitually] before Me [with integrity, knowing that you are always in My presences], and be blameless and complete [in obedience to Me].

April 15

God knows your innermost thoughts and feelings. Ask Him daily to sweep your heart clean and fill you with His Spirit.

Psalm 51:6

6 Behold, you desire truth in the innermost being,
And in the hidden part [of my heart] You will make me know wisdom.

April 16

When you feel most unloved, most abandoned, God's love is there. These are the times to wait, expecting humans or material gods to fill the void, and turn to He who never changes. His promises will never change, trust Him and claim the promise He sends to you.

Psalm 117

1 O praise the Lord, all your nations!
Praise Him, all you people!
2 For His lovingkindness prevails over us [and we triumph and overcome through Him],
And the truth of the Lord endures forever.
Praise the Lord! (Hallelujah!)

April 17

You have eternal life. Pause and let that sink in. God's grace through Jesus' death and resurrection promises a life with Him forever. Can you ever do enough to thank Him? Praise Him today and let the spirit shine through you.

Psalm 118:27-20

17 I will not die, but live,
And declare the works and recount the illustrious acts of the Lord.
18 The Lord has disciplined me severely,
But He has not given me over to death.
19 Open to me the [temple] gates of righteousness;
I shall enter through them; I shall give thanks to the Lord.
20 This is the gate of the Lord;
The righteous will enter through it.

April 18

Christians everywhere are facing persecution, from cultural oppression to death. Even in our own country, attempts are being made to silence our voice. We are called to be brave and live out our witness. As Joshua was told, be brave, God is with us.

1 Peter 5:8-9

8 Be sober [well balanced and self-disciplined], be alert and cautious at all times. That enemy of yours, the devil, prowls around like a roaring lion [fiercely hungry], seeking someone to devour. 9 But resist him, be firm in your faith [against his attack—rooted, established, immovable], knowing that the same experiences of suffering are being experienced by your brothers and sisters throughout the world. [You do not suffer alone.]

April 19

We design the face and personality we choose to share with the world. We want to be perceived in a certain way, to earn respect, love – whatever we think we need. But God knows our hearts, He knows our thoughts, and He loves us anyway.

Jeremiah 17:10

10 "I, the Lord, search and examine the mind,
I test the heart,
To give to each man according to his ways,
According to the results of his deeds.

April 20

East Tennessee is a wonderful place to see the work of the Creator year-round. How can His existence be questioned when you see a beautiful autumn leaf display in the Smokies? Look to the mountains and praise Him!

Psalm 121:1-21

1 I will lift up my eyes to the hills [of Jerusalem]—
From where shall my help come?
2 My help comes from the Lord
Who made heaven and earth.

April 21

When God calls you to do something, He already has it planned out, including the resources and strength you will need to complete it. He has an answer for each objection and shakes His head at all the "but's". Just do it. Rest in the peace of work done for Him.

Jeremiah 1:7

7 But the Lord said to me,
"Do not say, `I am [only] a young man,'
Because everywhere I send you, you shall go,
And whatever I command you, you shall speak.

April 22

In the midst of the evil that flourishes today, we must be beacons of good, shining against the darkness. God is our energy source, strengthening us in this task. Shine for your Father today.

Amos 5:14-15

14 Seek (long for, require) good and not evil, that you may live;
And so, may the Lord God of host be with you,
Just as you have said!
15 Hate evil and love good,
And establish justice in the [court of the city] gate.
Perhaps the Lord God of hosts
Will be gracious to the remnant of Joseph [that is, those who remain after God's judgement].

April 23

The concept of a Genesis week means starting fresh, looking at life in a new way, living in a new way, as Genesis 9 tells of a new creation. Today's scripture is long, but it lists the qualities of God's character. Begin your Genesis week by meditation on and thanking God for His steadfast love.

Psalm 103

1 Bless and affectionately praise the LORD, *O my soul,*
And all that is [deep] within me, bless His holy name.
2 Bless and affectionately praise the LORD, *O my soul,*
And do not forget any of His benefits;
3 Who forgives all your sins,
Who heals all your diseases;

4 Who redeems your life from the pit,
Who crowns you [lavishly] with lovingkindness and tender mercy;
5 Who satisfies your years with good things,
So that your youth is renewed like the [soaring] eagle.
6 The LORD *executes righteousness*
And justice for all the oppressed.
7 He made known His ways [of righteousness and justice] to Moses,
His acts to the children of Israel.
8 The LORD *is merciful and gracious,*
Slow to anger and abounding in compassion and lovingkindness.
9 He will not always strive with us,
Nor will He keep His anger forever.
10 He has not dealt with us according to our sins [as we deserve],
Nor rewarded us [with punishment] according to our wickedness.
11 For as the heavens are high above the earth,
So great is His lovingkindness toward those who fear and worship Him [with awe-filled respect and deepest reverence].
12 As far as the east is from the west,
So far has He removed our transgressions from us.
13 Just as a father loves his children,

So the LORD *loves those who fear and worship Him [with awe-filled respect and deepest reverence].*
14 For He knows our [mortal] frame;
He remembers that we are [merely] dust.
15 As for man, his days are like grass;
Like a flower of the field, so he flourishes.
16 For the wind passes over it and it is no more,
And its place knows it no longer.
17 But the lovingkindness of the LORD *is from everlasting to everlasting on those who [reverently] fear Him,*
And His righteousness to children's children,
18 To those who honor and keep His covenant,
And remember to do His commandments [imprinting His word on their hearts].
19 The LORD *has established His throne in the heavens,*
And His sovereignty rules over all [the universe].
20 Bless the LORD*, you His angels,*
You mighty ones who do His commandments,
Obeying the voice of His word!
21 Bless the LORD*, all you His hosts,*
You who serve Him and do His will.
22 Bless the LORD*, all you works of His, in all places of His dominion;*
Bless and affectionately praise the LORD*, O my soul!*

April 24

The Levites were called to service in the temple. They were "set apart" for that ministry. When you accepted Jesus as your savior, you were set apart just as the Levites for ministry in the "temple" where God has placed you. Reflect on how you are carrying out your service today.

Numbers 16:9

9 does it seem but a small thing to you that the God of Israel has separated you from the congregation of Israel, to bring you near to Himself, to do the service of the tabernacle of the Lord, and to stand before the congregation to minister to them;

April 25

God has gifted each of us with a special talent, our own unique way to serve Him. It may take some time to discover, but it is within us, placed there by God. Don't look at others and envy their gifts; rejoice in how special you are to the Father that He gave you your very own spiritual gift.

1 Peter 4:10

10 Just as each one of you has received a special gift [a spiritual talent, an ability graciously given by God], employ it in serving one another as [is appropriate for] good stewards of God's multi-faceted grace [faithfully using the diverse, varied gifts and abilities granted to Christians be God's unmerited favor].

April 26

In a job, we can find ourselves working to please a boss, advance ourselves, or hating to set foot in a workplace. Work is honorable, given by God to sustain us, and to honor Him with our attitude and witness. Check yourself today; how do you serve? And this is not confined to paid employment. Are you honoring Him with your service in the home?

Colossians 3:23-24

23 Whatever you do [whatever your task may be], work from the soul [that is, put in you very best effort], as [something done] for the Lord and not for men, 24 knowing [with all certainty that it is from the Lord [not from men] that you will receive the inheritance which is you [greatest] reward. It is the Lord Christ whom you [actually] serve.

April 27

Jesus gave us a perfect example of a servant's heart. Humbling ourselves and placing others first can be one of the hardest tasks our flesh takes on, but the rewards are both immediate and heavenly.

Mark 10:45

45 For even the Son of Man did not come to be served, but to serve, and to give His life as a ransom for many.

April 28

How many times do we fret and stew over a problem or circumstance in our lives, forgetting that the King of creation is beside us, ready to guide us and to air in our behalf? If we seek Him and His will first, then peace will exist in our hearts, and in our lives. Have Faith.

Psalm 145:18-19

18 The Lord is near to all who call on Him,
To all who call on Him in truth (without guile).
19 He will fulfill the desire of those who fear and worship Him [with awe-inspired reverence and obedience];
He also will hear their cry and will save them.

April 29

At times, we can grow discouraged in our work for the Lord, feeling that it goes unnoticed and unappreciated. But God sees, God knows, and someday He will show us how much it was worth in eternity.

Malachi 3:16

16 The those who feared the Lord [with awe-filled reverence] spoke to one another; and the Lord paid attention and heard it, and a book of remembrance was written before Him of those who fear the Lord [with an attitude of reverence and respect] and who esteem His name.

April 30

Just because a preacher, evangelist, or Bible teacher has a large following does not guarantee that he or she is teaching true scripture. God has warned us to watch for false prophets. Ask for wisdom, listen carefully, and search the word to discern what is real. Never just accept; verify.

1 John 4:1

1 Beloved do not believe every spirit [speaking through a self-proclaimed prophet]; instead test the spirits to see whether they are from God, because many false prophets and teachers have gone out into the world.

May 1

Jesus was speaking to the religious leaders in today's scripture, but we can all learn from the words. We can all use a little heart cleaning at times, getting rid of pride, envy, idols... Whatever intrudes or keeps us from the Lord's work. Clean a little today.

Matthew 12:34

34 You brood of vipers; how can you speak good things when you are evil? For the mouth speaks out of that which fills the heart.

May 2

A change of attitude can affect our mood and outlook. Concentrating on negative circumstances and problems causes us to be angry, and unable to think or move out of the present. God instructs us to rejoice at all times, to have an "attitude of gratitude." resolving to be positive, to see the good, lifts us above our circumstances, which are, after all, temporary. Rejoice today! Praise Him!

1 Thessalonians 5:16-17

16 Rejoice always and delight in your faith;
17 be unceasing and persistent in prayer;

May 3

We sometimes yearn for clean instruction to guide us through the pitfalls of life. We thrash around, slip and slide, and careen our way, usually with less than optimum results. Wouldn't it be easier to turn to God's word, place our hand in His, and let Him lead us?

Joshua 1:8

8 This Book of the law shall not depart from your mouth, but you shall read [and meditated on] it day and night, so that you may be careful to do [everything] in accordance with all that is written in it; for then you will make your way prosperous, and then you will be successful.

May 4

Being an ambassador for Christ is not a burden or challenge; it is a joy! We can never praise Him enough or glorify His name to others too many times. Let Him shine through you today!

2 Corinthians 5:19-20

19 that is, that God was in Christ reconciling the world to Himself, not counting people's sins against them [but canceling them]. And He has committed to us the message of reconciliation [that is, restoration to favor with God].

20 So we are ambassadors for Christ, as though God were making His appeal through us; we [as Christ's representatives] plead with you on behalf of Christ to be reconciled to God.

May 5

While we usually don't have family altars in our homes these days, Anna Graham Lotz suggests that we have a place where we gather our devotional materials, Bible, and journal together, and dedicate that place to our quiet time. Dedicate a place today for your special time with God for He is worthy.

Genesis 35:3

3 then let us get up and go up to Bethel, and I will make and alter there to God, who answered me in the day of my distress and has been with me wherever I have gone.

May 6

God loves to hear our praise. He hears our problems and desires, and pays close attention to our intercession, but nothing pleases Him more than our praise, even in the midst of our trails! Lift your voice to Him today!

Psalm 89:1

1 I will sing of the goodness and lovingkindness of the Lord forever; with my mouth, I will make know Your faithfulness from generation to generation.

May 7

When God planned your life, He planned what you would need to perform the tasks He has for you. When He calls you, the tools are ready for you to access, you need only ask. Be excited about your work, you have all you need.

Hebrews 13:20-21

20 Now may the God of peace [the source of serenity and spiritual well-being] who brought up from the dead out Lord Jesus, the great Shepherd of the sheep, through the blood that sealed and ratified the eternal covenant,

21 equip you with every good thing to carry out His will and strengthen you [making you complete and perfect as you ought to be], accomplishing in us that which is pleasing in His sight, through Jesus Christ, to whom be the glory forever and ever. Amen.

May 8

The most precious promise we have from God aside from eternal life is that He will never leave or forsake us. The God of creation is by our side eternally. What can this world do to us with such a Father and protector as He?

Deuteronomy 31:6

6 Be strong and courageous, do not be afraid or tremble in dread before them, for it is the Lord your God who does with you. He will not fail you or abandon you.

May 9

More than ever before, Christians must be on guard against false prophets. A message may be eloquent, and the speaker strong, but are Biblical principles being truthfully included? Does glory go to God or to the speaker? Test everything against the Word of God and stand strong.

Ezekiel 2:6

6 And you, son of man, neither fear them nor fear their words; though briars and thorns are all around you and you sit among scorpions, neither fear their words nor be dismayed at their presences, for they are a rebellious house.

May 10

No trial here on earth can touch our eternity. We have God's word on that. As with Shadrach, Meshach, and Abednego, He walks with us through the fire, and leads us out unscathed. Praise Him for His never-ending faithfulness and love.

Isaiah 43:2

*2 "When you pass through the waters, I will be with you;
And through the rivers, they will not overwhelm you.
When you walk through fire, you will not be scorched,
Nor will the flame burn you.*

May 11

Our focus is bringing honor and glory to Christ. We must be last, so He is first. Sometimes the accolades and rewards of this world distract us, and we get a "big head". Ask God to monitor your thinking and alert you when He moves to second place.

Psalm 40:16

16 Let all who seek You rejoice and be glad in You;
Let those who love Your salvation say continually,
"The Lord be magnified!"

May 12

Today's scripture list five qualities that are essential for the peace that a Christian life is centered upon. God is true to His word, He cannot lie, and cannot contradict Himself. Those facts make it easy to put those qualities into action.

Jeremiah 17:7

7 Blessed [with spiritual security] is the man wo believes and trusts in and relies on the Lord
And whose hope and confident expectation is the Lord.

May 13

Our best life comes from a relationship with Jesus. His love fills us, and His spirit guides us to fulfillment in His plan for us. He never leaves. Praise Him!

Psalm 16:11

11 You will show me the path of life;
In Your presence is fullness of joy;
In Your right hand, there are pleasures forevermore.

May 14

God formed man from clay, common and ordinary. But, into that clay, He breathed His own breath of life, holy and eternal. As you breathe, consider that you are infused with your Father's spirit and breath.

"I'm just a little dust person, infused with the breath of God." – Ann Graham Lotz.

Psalm 64:8

8 So they will be caused to stumble;
Their own tongue is against them;
All who gaze at them will shake the head [in scorn].

May 15

When we accept Jesus as our savior, He tells us that we are a new creation in Him. But it doesn't stop there. Until we go home to Him, we are constantly renewed, polished, and refined in the process of our sanctification. He is at work on you today; look for the results!

Psalm 104:30

You send out Your Spirit, they are created;
You renew the face of the ground.

May 16

Renewal in Christ comes daily, if we seek it. We can be constantly washed clean, and start fresh, when we trust Him to do His work within us. Remember, repent, repeat.

Psalm 51:10-12

10 Create in me a clean heart, O God,
And renew a right and steadfast spirit within me.
11 Do not cast me away from Your presence
And do not take Your Holy Spirit from me.
12 Restore to me the joy of Your salvation
And sustain me with a willing spirit.

May 17

Our attitude doesn't depend on outward influences. We can determine our mood by what we set our thoughts on. Perhaps the easiest game changer is praise, an attitude of grace and gratitude that thanks God for the blessings we receive each day, and for His steadfast love through trials. Set your thoughts above.

Proverbs 15:15

15 All the days of the afflicted are bad,
But a glad heart has a continual feast [regardless of the circumstances].

May 18

When you are sowing seeds for God, apply the principles of mercy and grace. Don't use the heavy hand of self-righteousness, or browbeat people into submission. Follow Christ's lead at all times. He will cultivate what you sow.

Hosea 10:12

12 Sow with a view to righteousness [that righteousness, like seed, may germinate]; Reap in accordance with mercy and lovingkindness.
Break up your uncultivated ground, for it is time to seek and search diligently for the Lord [and to long for His blessing] Until He comes to rain righteousness and His gift of salvation on you.

May 19

The Bible speaks to us as freshly today as when first read, so many thousands of years ago. Its truth is eternal. Stay in the word, and let its light guide your life.

Joshua 1:8

8 This Book of the Law shall not depart from your mouth, but you shall read [and meditate on] it day and night so that you may be careful to do [everything] in accordance with all that is written in it; for then you will make your way prosperous, and then you will be successful.

May 20

Focus is necessary to achieve any goal. When we come before the Lord, we need to focus on our attitude and our heart. Come seeking knowledge and wisdom and come to praise. You will leave full.

Ecclesiastes 5:1-2

1 Guard your steps and focus on what you are doing as you go to the house of God and draw near to listen rather than to offer the [careless or irreverent] sacrifice of fools; for they are too ignorant to know they are doing evil. 2 Do not be hasty with your mouth [speaking careless works vows] or impulsive in thought to bring up a matter before God. For God is in heaven and you are on earth; therefore, let your words be few.

May 21

God is alive. This fact separates Christianity from all the other religions in the world. Death has been conquered and the grave is empty. Your God is alive and able. Hallelujah!

Remember this scripture was uttered by Job while in the depths of despair.

Job 19:25

*25 "For I know that my Redeemer and Vindicator lives,
And at the last He will take His stand upon the earth.*

May 22

A common mistake we make is to view God in earthy terms, with emotions and thoughts like ours. But God cannot be boxed into our small definitions and cannot be limited to our views of power. He is all powerful, and all knowing; acknowledge His leadership today, and do not limit Him.

Psalm 92:5

*5 How great are Your works, O Lord!
Your thoughts are very deep [beyond man's understanding].*

May 23

Rocks are strong impenetrable, and lasting. When God is compared to a rock, the comparison carries those qualities with it. He is stronger than anything we face. Sin cannot penetrate Him and lies cannot cover His truth. He will stand when all else crumbles and falls away. Trust Him with your all today.

Psalm 92:15

15 [they are living memorials] to declare that the Lord is up right and faithful [to His promises]; He is my rock, and there is no unrighteousness in Him.

May 24

Make calling out to the Lord a habit. Don't let worry fester inside. Take it to Him and release it. Know the peace He can give.

Psalm 3:4-5

4 With my voice I was crying to the Lord,
And He answered me from His holy mountain. ---Selah.
5 I lay down and slept [safely];
I awakened, for the Lord sustains me.

May 25

Fear should not be part of a Christian's life. God Himself is with us, in all His majesty and power. Ask Him to calm your spirit and put your fears to rest. He holds you in His hand.

Isaiah 41:10

10 `Do not fear [anything], for I am with you;
Do not be afraid, for I am your God.
I will strengthen you, be assured I will help you;
I will certainly take hold of you with My righteous right hand [a hand of justice, of power, of victory, or salvation].'

May 26

God's timeline is not our own. We must be patient, in trust, knowing He is at work continually. He desires and know the best for us, and that may mean laying our plans down, and resting in His arms.

2 Peter 3:9

9 The Lord does not delay [as though He were unable to act] and is not slow about His promise, as some count slowness, but is [extraordinarily] patient toward you, not wishing for any to perish but for all to come to repentance.

May 27

God delights in you! The creator of the universe dotes on you! Never let anyone tell you that you have no worth; you are God's child!

Psalm 18:19

19 He brought me out into a broad place;
He rescued me because He was pleased with me and delighted in me.

May 28

Society values a busy life, crammed full of activities, seeing that as more valuable. But God calls us to times of solitude and quiet, actively listening for His voice. Begin achieving that balance in your life today.

Psalm 46:10

10 "Be still and know (recognize, understand) that I am God.
I will be exalted among the nations! I will be exalted in the earth."

May 29

A habit we fall into is gaining the approval of others. Given work evaluations, close friends, and family relationships, it comes naturally. But we are to do everything for God's favor. Do we do that? Practice that today, and let all others fall away. Work for Him.

Galatians 1:10

10 Am I now trying to win the favor and approval of men, or of God? Or am I seeking to please someone? If I were still trying to be popular with men, I would not be a bond-servant of Christ.

May 30

When you keep your eyes focused on God, no work is unrewarding. He places you in situations and places where He can use you for His purpose; serving Him is its own reward. Strive to please Him.

Colossians 3:22-25

22 Servants, in everything obey those who are your masters on earth, not only with external service, as those who merely please people, but with sincerity of heart because of your fear of the Lord. 23 Whatever you do [whatever your task may be], work from the soul [that is, put in your very best effort], as [something done] for the Lord and not for men, 24 knowing [with all certainty] that it is from the Lord [not from men] that you will receive the inheritance which is your [greatest] reward. It is the Lord Christ whom you [actually] serve. 25 For he who does wrong will be punished for his wrongdoing, and [with God] there is no partiality [no special treatment based on a person's position in life].

May 31

God allows everything that happens to us. There is a purpose, refining us to conform closer and closer to Christ's image. We may not understand some things or events, but we can always be grateful for what He has done, and for what is waiting for us.

1 Thessalonians 5:18

18 In every situation [no matter what the circumstances] be thankful and continually give thanks to God; for this is the will of God for you in Christ Jesus.

June 1

There is so much to be glad about when you're a child of the King! Don't be mired down in temporary circumstances, turn your heart and voice to praise and raise your eyes heavenward.

Psalm 59: 16-17

16 But as for me, I will sing of Your mighty strength and power;
Yes, I will sing joyfully of Your lovingkindness in the morning;
For You have been my stronghold
And a refuge in the day of my distress.
17 To You, O [God] my strength, I will sing praises;
For God is my stronghold [my refuge, my protector, my high tower],
The God who shows me [steadfast] lovingkindness.

June 2

God's love for you is everlasting. Never forget or doubt. Trust Him and take everything to Him.

Jeremiah 31:3

3 The Lord appeared to me (Israel) from ages past, saying,
"I have loved you with an everlasting love;
Therefore, with lovingkindness I have drawn you and continued My faithfulness to you.

June 3

There is no trouble, no circumstances, that God cannot pick you up, shelter you, and restore you. Trust Him. Cry out to Him.

Psalm 27:5

5 For in the day of trouble He will hide me in His shelter;
In the secret place of His tent He will hide me;
He will lift me up on a rock.

June 4

God is always at work in and on you, precious child. Even when we feel most alone, He is right there, waiting to show you what you are learning in this time. Never lose that promise and hope.

Philippians 1:6

6 I am convinced and confident of this very thing, that He who has begun a good work in you will [continue to] perfect and complete it until the day of Christ Jesus [the time of His return].

June 5

We spend a lot of time crying out to God "why" wanting reasons and information about circumstances and trials. We do this even though we have a book that tells us about His love, His character, and His constant care for us. Rest on what you know, and trust that it will all be revealed when it is time.

Deuteronomy 29:29

29 "The secret things belong to the Lord our God, but the tings which are revealed and disclosed belong to us and to our children forever, so that we may do all of the words of this law.

June 6

It seems as if Satan has taken over the world. Evil is everywhere in the hearts of men. But today's scripture tells us that even the demons are under the dominion of God. Take heart; these times are temporary, and God remains on the throne for eternity.

Mark 5:12-13

12 And the demons begged Him, saying, "send us to the pigs so that we may go into them!" 13 Jesus gave them permission. And the unclean spirits came out [of the man] and entered the pigs. The herd, numbering about two thousand, rushed down the steep bank into the sea; and they were drowned [one after the other] in the sea.

June 7

Fear is a crippling emotion, and taken to the extreme, can lead to life-crippling anxiety. Take your fear captive, and hand it over to Christ; His power overcomes fear forever. Do not fear.

Mark 5:36

36 Overhearing what was being said, Jesus said to the synagogue official, "Do not be afraid; only keep on believing [in Me and my power]."

June 8

Someday we will dwell with God; that means see Him, talking with Him, sharing a forever home. Let that certain knowledge sustain you today and carry you through whatever you face.

Psalm 27:4

4 One thing I have asked of the Lord, and that I will seek:
That I may dwell in the house of the Lord [in His presence] all the days of my life,
To gaze upon the beauty [the delightful loveliness and majestic grandeur] of the Lord
And to meditate in His temple.

June 9

God's supplies of grace, mercy, and love are limitless. The well never runs dry. Our human mind cannot grasp that fact, but out faith can believe and trust.

Lamentations 3:22-23

*22 It is because of the Lord's lovingkindness that we are nor consumed,
Because His [tender] compassions never fail.
23 They are new every morning;
Great and beyond measure is Your Faithfulness.*

June 10

God stands ready to guide us with Hs eternal wisdom and love. Take your dilemmas and cares to Him and resist the urge to act on your own. Let Him make the decisions.

Proverbs 2:6-8

*6 For the Lord gives [skillful and godly] wisdom;
From His mouth come knowledge and understanding.
7 He stores away sound wisdom for the righteous [those who are in right standing with Him];
He is a shield to those who walk in integrity [those of honorable character and moral courage],
8 He guards that paths of justice;
And He preserves the way of His Saints (believers).*

June 11

The spiritual nourishment we receive from God's "food" (His word and our time with Him in prayer) sustains us more than anything the world can offer. Let your "diet" center around seeking Him and be filled with satisfaction and joy.

Psalm 34:8-10

8 O taste and see that the Lord [our God] is good;
How blessed [fortunate, prosperous, and favored by God] is the man who takes refuge in Him.
9 O [reverently] fear the Lord, you His saints (believers, holy ones);
For to those who fear Him there is no want.
10 The young lions lack [food] and grow hungry,
But they who seek the Lord will not lack any good thing.

June 12

God hears our cries to Him. We don't have to be perfect, or super spiritual, or church leaders. We are His children, and that's enough. Turn to Him today.

Psalm 27:7

Hear, O Lord, when I cry aloud;
Be gracious and compassionate to me and answer me.

June 13

The Father, Son, and Holy Spirit, while one, are three distinct entities that function to perform the Father's will, in our lives and in our world. We call on each at different times according to what we are feeling but each promises the love and care of God. Be thankful for the Trinity's active presences in your life.

Isaiah 32:2

*2 Each [one of them] will be like a hiding place from the wind
And a shelter from the storm,
Like streams of water in a dry land,
Like the shade of a huge rock in a parched and weary land [to those who turn to them].*

June 14

Christ gives us a spirit of generosity. He has done so much for us, and loves us, so we want to pass it on. Greed and stinginess have no part in your life as a Christ-follower. Let streams of love and blessing flow from your heart originating from God's love.

Psalm 112:5

*5 It is well with the man who is gracious and lends;
He conducts his affairs with justice.
Proverbs 11:25
25 The generous man [is a source of blessing and] shall be prosperous and enriched,
And he who waters will himself be watered [reaping the generosity he has sown].*

June 15

Carefully examine the way you feel about money and possessions. Do they hold you hostage, or are they a means to show love to others? Nothing in this world will last but God's love is eternal. Reflect this to those around you, giving God first place in everything.

1 Timothy 6:17-19

17 As for the rich in this present world, instruct them not to be conceited and arrogant, nor to set their hope on the uncertainty of riches, but on God, who richly and ceaselessly provides us with everything for our enjoyment. 18 instruct them to do good, to be rich in good works, to be generous, willing to share [with others]. 19 In this way storing up for themselves the enduring riches of good foundation for the future, so that they may take hold of that which is truly life.

June 16

In all circumstances, our first response should always be seeking the voice of the Lord for guidance and His wisdom. Never tackle life under your own power; look to the Author and Defender of our faith.

Psalm 86:7

*7 In the day of my trouble I will call upon You,
For You will answer me.*

June 17

God's blessings come free and clear; no strings attached. Celebrate your generous Father today and accept His grace.

Proverbs 10:22

22 The blessing of the Lord brings [true] riches,
And He adds no sorrow to it [for it comes as a blessing from God].

June 18

We may not understand some circumstances that happen in our lives, but we have a God that we can turn to for strength, protection, and endless love. He is truly our rock.

Psalm 61

1 Hear my cry, O God;
Listen to my prayer.
2 From the end of the earth I call to You, when my heart is overwhelmed and weak;
Lead me to the rock that is higher than I [a rock that is too high to reach without Your help].
3 For You have been a shelter and a refuge for me,
A strong tower against the enemy.
4 Let me dwell in Your tent forever;
Let me take refuge in the shelter of Your wings. --- Selah.
5 For You have heard my vows, O God;
You have given me the inheritance of those who fear Your name [with reverence].
6 You will prolong the king's life [adding days upon days];
His years will be like many generations.
7 He will sit enthroned forever before [the face of] God;
appoint lovingkindness and truth to watch over and preserve him.
8 So I will sing praise to Your name forever,
Paying my vows day by day.

June 19

To reach our full potential in our walk with Christ, we must be willing to be shaped by Him. We must submit to His guidance and to His refining, and watch for what He is teaching us, to be His clay.

Isaiah 64:8

8 Yet, O Lord, You are our Father;
We are the clay, and You our Potter,
And we all are the work of Your hand.

June 20

Where do you find your joy? Scripture tells us that those who delight in the Lord and His work will never lack for joy and peace. Resolve to seek your joy there.

Psalm 1:1-2

1 Blessed [fortunate, prosperous, and favored by God] is the man who does not walk in the counsel of the wicked [following their advice and example],
Nor stand in the path of sinners,
Nor sit [down to rest] in the seat of scoffers (ridiculer).
2 But his delight is in the law of the Lord,
And on His law [His precepts and teachings] he [habitually] mediates day and night.

June 21

God is never far away. If we call to Him with our hearts, He hears, and is closer than anyone could be. Seek Him today.

Jeremiah 29:13

13 Then [with a deep longing] you will seek Me and require Me [as a vital necessity] and [you will] find Me when you search for Me with all your heart.

June 22

We can trust Jesus with our cares. He doesn't gossip, or otherwise betray your trust. You can unburden all to Him, knowing He will listen, and will guide you through your trials. Talk to Him.

1 Peter 5:7

7 Casting all your cares [all your anxieties, all your worries, and all your concerns, once and for all] on Him, for He cares about you [with deepest affection, and watches over you very carefully].

June 23

Jesus has set us free; from sin, from the flesh, from death. Nothing has a claim on us, save our Father's love. Never let anything less take you hostage. Rejoice!

John 8:36

36 So is the Son makes you free, then you are unquestionable free.

June 24

God has brought you into the light of His love, and in doing so, broke the chains of fleshy bondage. But the flesh does not give up easily. Ask God to reveal where bondage still exists and ask for His power to rise above it.

Psalm 107:14

14 He brought them out of darkness and the deep (deathly) darkness And broke their bonds apart.

June 25

Being human, we tend to place our trust in things and people. But eventually, these will let us down, and disappoint us. God never will. Rely on Him for your foundation, guidance, and love. Trust Him.

Psalm 4:8

8 In peace [and with a tranquil heart] I will both lie down and sleep, For You alone, O Lord, make me dwell in safety and confident trust.

June 26

Today, ask for the ability to see others through Jesus' eyes. He had compassion for all people, knowing they were created in His image, even though they might not reflect that. He knew what it was to be judged on the surface.

1 Peter 2:4

4 Come to Him [the risen Lord] as to a living Stone which men rejected and threw away, but which is choice and precious in the sight of God.

June 27

Sometimes we feel the walls caving in, and we are alone and scared. But feelings can lie; we are never alone, and we can turn our fears over to our Father. Reach out and touch His hand. He will sustain you.

Psalm 27:12

*12 Do not give me up to the will of my adversaries,
For false witnesses, have come against me;
They breathe out violence.*

June 28

God desires all of us. We tend to hold some parts of ourselves back, or some possessions or money. Search your heart and mind and let the Spirit prompt you to find the areas where God is not honored or in control.

Deuteronomy 10:12-13

12 "And now, Israel, what does the Lord God require from you, but to fear [and worship] the Lord your God [with awe-filled reverence and profound respect], to walk [that is, to live each and every day] in all His ways and to love Him, and to serve the Lord your God with all your heart and with all your soul [your choices, your thoughts, your whole being], 13 and to keep the commandments of the Lord and His statutes which I am commanding you today for your good?

June 29

Jesus opens our eyes and hearts to teach us what He wants us to know. He loves us and wants to share in our learning experience. Be watching today for what He has planned for you to see and to understand. Delight in the relationship with your Father.

John 15:11

11 I have told you these things so that MY joy and delight may be in you, and that your joy may be made full and complete and overflowing.

June 30

We are made in Christ's image, to reflect Him to the world. Be conscious of that, always striving to live your faith in front of others seeking to draw them to Him. Be authentically Christian.

Titus 2:7-8

7 And in all things, show yourself to be an example of good works, with purity in doctrine [having the strictest regard for integrity and truth], dignified, 8 sound and beyond reproach in instruction, so that the opponent [of the faith] will be shamed, having nothing bad to say about us.

July 1

God doesn't just tell us not to fear, He commands us. When we walk in Christ, we fear nothing because we are with the Creator ad ruler of everything. Be courageous today.

Joshua 1:9

9 Have I not commanded you? Be strong and courageous! Do not be terrified or dismayed (intimidated), for the Lord your God is with you wherever you go."

July 2

When you become a Christian, God establishes the covenant of adoption with you. He will never forget you, forsake you, or quit loving you. This is forever trust Him and take Him at His word.

1 Chronicles 16:14-15

*14 He is the Lord our God;
His judgments are in all the earth.
15 Be mindful of His covenant forever,
The promise which He commanded and established
To a thousand generations*

July 3

It's hard on this earth, and we have the tears and the bruises to prove it. But, as we persevere with our hand in Jesus' sacred hand, we see ahead to the joy and delight at the future destination. What hope we have!

Psalm 126:5-6

5 They who sow in tears shall reap with joyful singing.
6 HE who does back and forth weeping, carrying his bag of seed [for planting],
Will indeed come again with a shout of joy, bringing his sheaves with him.

July 4

Just as God must be the foundation of your own life, He must be the foundation of your home. Ask Him about any decisions that must be made; invite Him to be an active participant in every day. Let your home be known as one that points to Christ.

Psalm 127:1

1 Unless the Lord builds the house,
They labor in vain who build it;
Unless the Lord guards the city,
The watchman keeps awake in vain.

July 5

In our fleshly lives, we instinctively lash out when others hurt us. If God reacted that way to us, we would be doomed. But His divine character and boundless love offer love and forgiveness time after time. Let Him search your life today for anyone you may need to forgive; emulate His example today.

Psalm 130:3-4

3 If You, Lord, should keep an account of our sins and treat us accordingly, O Lord, who could stand [before you in judgement and claim innocence]?

4 But there is forgiveness with You,
That You may be feared and worshiped [with submissive wonder].

July 6

God tells us His work will accomplish what He intends it to do. So, if you are feeling discouraged, frozen, or feeling helpless, look into the Bible and pray God's promises to Him. Turn loose His power.

Isaiah 55:11

11 So will My word be which goes out of My mouth;
It will not return to Me void (useless, without result),
Without accomplishing what I desire,
And without succeeding in the matter for which I sent it.

July 7

God tells us many times in His word not to fear, but do we really obey that command? He stands ready to fulfill His promises to be all we need, to be our strength, and to be our father. Grasp hold of this today.

Psalm 46:1-3

1 God is our refuge and strength [mighty impenetrable],
A very present and well-proved help in trouble.
2 Therefore we will not fear, though the earth should change
And though the mountains be shaken and slip into the heart of the seas,
3 Though its waters roar and foam,
Though the mountains tremble at its roaring.

July 8

In ancient times, a seat to the right of the host indicated prestige and honor. Today's Scripture portrays God at our right hand, in the most honored place in our lives. Meditate on your life and see if that is where you seat Him.

Psalm 16:8

8 I have set the Lord continually before me;
Because He is at my right hand, I will not be shaken.

July 9

Fear is a real human emotion, but God does not want His children to be fearful. He wants us to understand that He is with us at all times, fighting for us and with us. Confess your fear to Him today and let Him fill you with courage.

Psalm 56:3-4

3 When I am afraid,
I will put my trust and faith in You
4 In God, whose word I praise;
In God, I have put my trust;
I shall not fear.
What can mere man do to me?

July 10

The most worthy action of a believer is to tell others of the saving grace and love of Christ. Often, you don't even need words; just witness by your life and actions. Be a light to the world today.

Isaiah 52:7

7 How beautiful and delightful on the mountains
Are the feet of him who brings good news,
Who announces peace,
Who brings good news of good [things],
Who announces salvation,
Who says to Zion, "Your God reigns!"

July 11

The love and strength of God is information to be shared with all around you. We don't keep it all to ourselves. Let His light shine through you so others see and ask why you are different. Then, tell them about your Savior.

Psalm 78:4

4 We will not hide them from their children, but [we will] tell to the generation to come the praiseworthy deeds of the Lord, and [tell of] His great might and power and the wonderful works that He has done.

July 12

Our country needs prayer. Our leaders need prayer. Our churches need prayer. Today, commit to be one person that will call for revival, renewal, and reason to reappear in America. Pray that God will start with you.

Daniel 9:18-19

18 O my God incline Your ear and hear; pen Your eyes and look at our desolations and the city which is call by Your name; for we are not presenting our supplications before You because of our own merits and righteousness, but because or Your great mercy and compassion. 19 O Lord, hear! O Lord, forgive! O Lord, listen and take action! Do not delay, for Your own sake, O my God, because Your city and Your people are called by Your name.

July 13

Society may creep into our minds, telling us that "he who has the most toys wins." But that's not God's blueprint for a meaningful Christian life. What we experience from a relationship with Him is far richer than any material gains on earth. Set your path according to His plan.

Proverbs 10:16

16 The wages of the righteous [the upright, those in right standing with God is [a worthwhile, meaningful] life, The income of the wicked, punishment.

July 14

Each day that you are walking and working in God's way, you are coming closer to being in the image of God. It is said that the glory of God is blinding; each day we are reflecting more of that glory. What a thought!

2 Corinthians 3:18

18 And we all, with unveiled face, continually seeing as in a mirror the glory of the Lord, are progressively being transformed into His image from [one degree or] glory to [even more] glory, which comes from the Lord, [who is] the Spirit.

July 15

Christ was fully human, as well as divine, and, as such was tempted just like us. He understands and is faithful to deliver us when we turn to Him. There is nothing you and He together cannot overcome.

1 Corinthians 10:13

13 No temptation [regardless of its source] has overtaken or enticed you that is not common to human experience [nor is any temptation unusual or beyond human resistance]; but God is faithful [to His word – He is compassionate and trustworthy], and He will not let you be tempted beyond your ability [to resist], but along with the temptation HE [has in the past and is not and] will [always] provide the way out as well, so that you will be able to endure it [without yielding, and will overcome temptation with joy].

July 16

A life lived for God is a life of Joy, for we know that no matter what, He is with us, and loves us. The work we do is an offering to Him, given out of that joy. Enjoy every Sabbath day.

Ecclesiastes 9:7-10

7 Go your way, eat your bread with joy and drink your wine with a cheerful heart [if you are righteous, wise, and in the hands of God]; for God has already approved and accepted your works. 8 Let your clothes always be white [with purity], and do not let the oil [of gladness] be lack on your head. 9 Live joyfully with the wife whom you love all the days of fleeting life which He has given you under the sun --- all the days of vanity and futility. For this is your reward in life and in your work in which you have labored under the sun. 10 What your hand finds to do, do it with all your might; for there is not activity or planning or knowledge or wisdom in sheol (the nether world, the place of the dead) where you are going.

July 17

Our ultimate aim in our Christian walk is to conform to the image of Christ. In the process, our minds are shaped more and more by His thoughts and His designs. Ask Him to reveal where and when your mind is influenced more by the world than by Him, and then submit to His gentle redirection.

Romans 15:5-6

5 Now may the God who gives endurance and who supplies encouragement grant the you be of the same mind with one another according to Christ Jesus, 6 So that with one accord you may with one voice glorify and praise and honor the God and Father of our Lord Jesus Christ.

July 18

Let your heart sing to the Lord today, in praise for all He has promised to you! You are His child, the treasure of His heart He walks with you and protects you. There is no greater joy on earth then living for Him.

1 Chronicles 16:22-23

*22 "Do not touch My anointed ones,
And do My prophets no harm."*

*23 Sing to the Lord, all the earth;
Proclaim the good news of His salvation from day to day.*

July 19

Take a moment to study the creation around you, the beauty in nature. Look up to the beautiful blue skies. Man did not make any of this. Only and almighty God, ruler of the universe, could speak this into existence. Surely, He can handle whatever you are dealing with.

1 Chronicles 16:25-27

25 For great is the Lord, and greatly to be praised; He is also to be feared [with awe-filled reverence] above all gods.

26 For all the gods of the peoples are [lifeless] idols, But the Lord made the heavens.

27 Splendor and majesty and [found] in His presence; Strength and joy are [found] in His place (sanctuary).

July 20

The key to waiting on the Lord is having confidence that He will answer, and that confidence come from remembering and resting on His promises, and that the answer will be according to His will.

Psalm 27: 13-14

13 I would have despaired had I not believed that I would see the goodness of the Lord In the land of the living.

14 Wait for and confidently expect the Lord;
Be strong and let your heart take courage;
Yes, wait for and confidently expect the Lord.

July 21

Aspire to living in such a way that people recognize there's a different motivation within you. Let them ask, and then share the hope you hold through Jesus. Let the spirit Glow within you. It begins with your surrender.

Colossians 1:4-5

4 For we have heard of your faith in Christ Jesus [how you lean on Him with absolute confidence in His power, wisdom, and goodness], and of the [unselfish] love which you have for all the saints (god's people); 5 because of the [confident] hope [of experiencing that] which is reserved and waiting for you in heaven. You previously heard of the hope in the message of truth, and the gospel [regarding salvation].

July 22

When someone goes before you, they lead you in the right direction, and clear the path so it is safe. They look out for you. God has promised this for you, and we can believe He will. Why fear any person or circumstance when God has been there before you?

Deuteronomy 31:8

8 It is the Lord who goes before you; He will be with you. He will not fail you or abandon you. Do not fear or be dismayed.

July 23

The Spirit often places a burden for someone on our hearts. Don't ignore it; God has commanded us to care for our neighbors He will equip you for the task He has given you and will give you enough love to cover all.

Romans 15:2

2 Let each one of us [make it a practice to] please his neighbor for his good, to build him up spiritually.

July 24

We work to become spiritually mature, growing in faith and in knowledge of our Father. In doing so, we not only know Him better, but become better equipped to fill our role in His Church. Pray for Him to fill you with thirst for His word and His work.

Ephesians 3:14-16

14 For this reason [grasping the greatness of this plan by which Jews and Gentiles are joined together in Christ] I bow my knees [in reverence] before the Father [of our Lord Jesus Christ], 15 from whom every family in heaven and on earth derives its name [God – the first and ultimate Father]. 16 May He grant you out of the riches of His glory, to be strengthened and spiritually energized with power through His Spirit in your inner self, [indwelling your innermost being and personality].

July 25

As we struggle through our day, meeting one hassle after another, we forget the unbelievable power of the Spirit that resides within us. So much bigger than anything we face, it gives us the boost we need to rise and to live above the fracas. Rely on that inner power source.

17 [I always pray] that the God of our Lord Jesus Christ, the Father of glory, may grant you a spirit of wisdom and of revelation [that gives you a deep and personal and intimate insight] into the true knowledge of Him [for we know the Father through the Son]. 18 And [I Pray] that the eyes of your heart [the very center and core of your being] may be enlightened [flooded with light by the Holy Spirit], so that your will know and cherish the hope [the divine guarantee, the confident expectation] to which He has called you, the riches of His glorious inheritance in the saints (God's people), 19 and [so that you will begin to know] what the immeasurable and unlimited and surpassing greatness of His [active, spiritual] power is in us who believe. These are in accordance with the working of His mighty strength.

July 26

If God calls you to something, He will equip and empower you. This doesn't mean you won't be tired, discouraged, and scared. It does mean you have an unending power sources, and you are not doing it all on your own.

Colossian 1:29

29 For this I labor [often to the point of exhaustion], striving with His power and energy, which so greatly works within me.

July 27

Today's Scripture contains the action verbs "protect" and "guard". Both convey the idea that you are surrounded 24/7 by an army ready to fight for you. And, that army is almighty, the Creator, God of the angel armies. How you are cherished and loved!

Psalm 121:7-8

7 The Lord will protect you from all evil; He will keep your life.
8 The Lord will guard your going out and your coming in [everything that you do] From this time forth and forever.

July 28

God promises that He is always with us in the good and the bad, in the flowers and the fire, in the peace and the turmoil. Our hearts can be calm, resting in His love.

Isaiah 43:2

2 "When you pass through the waters, I will be with you;
And through the rivers, they will not overwhelm you.
When you walk through fire, you will not be scorched,
Nor will the flame burn you.

July 29

Always keep your eyes and your focus turned upwards concentrating on God and acknowledging His power and control. Satan loves to distract us, causing us to look around and search other places for answers. Keep alert to his tactics, and resist. Your solutions are seated in God.

Psalm 121:1

1 I will lift up my eyes to the hills [of Jerusalem] ---
From where shall my help come?

July 30

When your problems seem insurmountable, remember the God who created the universe is at your right hand ready to move that universe for His child. He will never leave you. He loves you.

Psalm 121:2

2 My help comes from the Lord,
Who made heaven and earth.

July 31

God has your life. That means no matter what, He is with you, and will bring you to Him when it is time. Just as we keep treasures safe here on earth, He keeps us safe for all eternity. Such love.

Psalm 121:7

7 The Lord will protect you from all evil;
HE will keep your life.

August 1

We are God's children, set apart for greater things. The world will not accept or approve of us, but we don't want that approval anyway. Aim to please God, and you will have peace within.

1 John 3:1

1 See what an incredible quality of love the Father has shown to us, that we would [be permitted to] be named and called and counted the children of God! And so we are! For this reason the world does not know us, because it did not know Him.

August 2

Live in expectation for what God is about to do. He promises new things are coming, but we need to be alert to see them. Don't let your wants cloud your vision. Wait on the Lord.

*18 "Do not remember the former things,
Or ponder the things of the past.
19 "Listen carefully, I am about to do a new thing,
Now it will spring forth;
Will you not be aware of it?
I will even put a road in the wilderness,
Rivers in the desert.*

August 3

Today's Scripture shows the two sides of our God; a mighty warrior and a gentle father. He fights for/with us and forgives us with equal might. Take a moment to meditate on this passage and praise Him for loving you so much.

Zephaniah 3:14-17

14 Shout for joy, O Daughter of Zion!
Shout in triumph, O Israel!
Rejoice, be in high spirits and glory with all your heart,
O daughter of Jerusalem [in that day]!
15 The Lord has taken away that judgments against you;
He has cleared away your enemies.
The king of Israel, even the Lord [Himself], is in your midst;
You will no longer fear disaster.
16 In that day it will be said to Jerusalem:
"Do not be afraid, O Zion;
Do not let your hands fall limp.
17 "The Lord your God is in your midst,
A warrior who saves.
He will rejoice over you with joy;
He will be quiet in His love [making no mention of your past sins],
He will rejoice over you with shouts of joy.

August 4

Sometimes, we momentarily forget that God is the great I Am. No one created Him or taught Him. He is the repository of all wisdom and knowledge. Our human condition makes it hard to grasp that concept, but we accept it in faith. Worship His greatness today in awe of His being.

Isaiah 40:13

*13 Who has directed the Spirit of the Lord,
Or has taught Him as His counselor?*

August 5

Jesus has trusted us with His word and His example. He considers us trustworthy and reliable. Remember this as you go through this day and the coming week. Would He be glad He put His trust in you?

2 Timothy 2:1-3

1 So you, my son, be strong [constantly strengthened] and empowered in the grace that is [to be found only] in Christ Jesus. 2 The things [doctrine, the precepts, that admonitions, the sum of my ministry] which you have heard me teach in the presence of many witnesses, entrust [as a treasure] to reliable and faithful men who will also be capable and qualified to teach others. 3 Take with me your share of hardship [passing through the difficulties which you are called to endure], like a good soldier of Christ Jesus.

August 6

When you received Christ as your Savior, you were ordained as one of His royal priesthood; what an honor and responsibility! Today, on this Lord's day, think about what that means for your life; take your "training" in church seriously, and thank Him for this privilege. Prepare for the mission week ahead.

1 Peter 2:9

9 But you are a chosen race, a royal priesthood, a consecrated nation, a [special] people for God's own possession, so that you may proclaim the excellences [the wonderful deeds and virtues and perfections] of Him who called you out of darkness into His marvelous light.

August 7

The princes and princesses of a monarchy are trained from birth on their behavior, manners, and deportment, so they represent the royal family in a positive way. You are the child of the greatest king of any ever known; He provided you with an example of behavior in Christ and gave you a manual to guide you, full of His Word. Study to make Him proud.

John 1:12

12 But to as many as did receive and welcome Him, He gave the right [the authority, the privilege] to become children of God, that is, to those who believe in (adhere to, trust in, and rely on) His name.

August 8

Sometimes the ugliest disagreements we have are with Christian friends. Imagine how this pains God to see His children squabbling and putting a bad example forward for others. Resolve today to put aside pettiness; bury the hatchet necessary and move forward with kingdom work.

Ephesians 4:3

3 Make every effort to keep the oneness of the Spirit in the bond of peace [each individual working together to make the whole successful].

August 9

The world's measure of worth is directly opposite God's. Sometimes we forget that surrounded as we are by other influences. But our Father is all powerful and is in control at all times. Keep your eyes and heart focused above.

Psalm 147:5-6

5 Great is our [majestic and mighty] Lord and abundant in strength;
His understanding is inexhaustible [infinite, boundless].
6 The Lord lifts up the humble;
He casts the wicked down to the ground.

August 10

God commands us to rejoice in all things, including sorrow, trials, and worries. He knows if we rejoice and lift our hearts in worship, our focus will return to Him, His plan for us, and our certainty of an eternal future with Him. Our home is not this earth; we are just "traveling through"

1 Thessalonians 5:16-18

16 Rejoice always and delight in your faith; 17 be unceasing and persistent in prayer; 18 in every situation [no matter what the circumstances] be thankful and continually give thanks to God; for this is the will of God for you in Christ Jesus.

August 11

Intellectually, we know that God created the world and everything in and around it. But sometimes we forget that He created us for Him. Each of us, individually, was designed and perfected by God for Him. He wanted you! Live that thought out today! You are special to God!

Colossians 1:16

16 For by Him all things were created in heaven and on earth, [things] visible and invisible, whether thrones or dominions or rulers or authorities; all things were created and exist through Him [that is, by His activity] and for Him.

August 12

Christ's work does not stop with our acceptance of salvation, and recognition of Him as our savior. At that time, the Trinity join together for our protection, and for our transformation. Take a moment to reflect on how you've grown since you were saved; then thank Him for what is yet to come.

1 Thessalonians 5:24

24 Faith and absolutely trustworthy is He who is calling you [to Himself for your salvation], and He will do it [He will fulfill His call by making you holy, guarding you, watching over you, and protecting you as His own].

August 13

Let the word fill your hearts and minds. Keep your overall focus on what God has said, promised, and fulfilled already. Nothing in this world will last, so concentrate on what is everlasting – God.

Deuteronomy 6:4-9

4 "Hear, O Israel! The Lord is our God; The Lord is one [the only God]! 5 You shall love the Lord your God with all your heart and mind and with all your soul and with all your strength [your entire being]. 6 These words, which I am commanding you today, shall be [written] on your heart and mind. 7 You shall teach them diligently to your children [impressing God's precepts on their minds and penetrating their hearts with His truths] and Shall speak of them when you get up. 8 And you shall bind them as a sign on your hand (forearm), and they shall be used as bands (frontals, frontlets) on your forehead. 9 You shall write them on the doorposts of your house and on your gates.

August 14

No matter how hard we try none of us can live a righteous life; our fleshly nature leads us to flirt with sin. But, keeping our hearts and minds on Christ reminds us where our power source and champion are, and we can turn the fight over to Him; we don't have to fight alone.

Romans 7:24-25

24 Wretched and miserable man that I am! Who will [rescue me and] set me free from this body of death [this corrupt, moral existence]? 25 Thanks be to God [for my deliverance] through Jesus Christ our Lord! So then, on the one hand I myself with my mind serve the law of God, but on the other, with my flesh [my human nature, my worldliness, my sinful capacity – I serve] the law of sin.

August 15

Sometimes it feels like God is not paying attention or has turned His back on earthly matters. Make no mistake; God's hand is on everything. He is in control and will someday make this known in a mighty way. Trust Him in everything.

Job 12:9-10

9 "Who among all these does not recognize [in all these things that good and evil are randomly scattered throughout nature and human life] That the hand of the Lord has done this,
10 In whose hand is the life of every living thing,
And the breath of all mankind?

August 16

In these unsteady, unsure, uneasy times, we can become fearful and anxious. But He is in control; give whatever burden you are carrying to Him, and trust in His strength. After all, He has already told you how the story ends.

Job 12:13-14

13 "But [only] with Him are [perfect] wisdom and might;
He [alone] has [true] counsel and understanding.
14 "Behold, He tears down, and it cannot be rebuilt;
He imprisons a man, and there can be no release.

August 17

The basic belief and truth of your life is the knowledge that your redeemer lives. He has conquered sin and death, and because of that, you are His child, and heir to an eternal home of love and grace. Now what are you facing that is bigger than your God?

Job 19:25

25 "For I know that me Redeemer and vindicator lives,
And at the last He will take His stand upon the earth.

August 18

Being a child of God corresponds to one of the closest relationships we have on earth, that of parent and child. It also parallels the emotions we experience in that relationship; great love, great anger, great pride, great disappointment. So, do not berate yourself when you have normal family emotions in your work with God. Just recognize that you and your father are growing closer, close enough to be honest in your feelings.

1 John 3:1-2

1 See what an incredible quality of love the Father has shown to us, that we would [be permitted to] be named and called and counted the children of God! And so, we are! For this reason, the world does not know us, because it did not know Him. 2 Beloved, we are [even here and] now children of God, and it is not yet made clear what we will be [after His coming]. We know that when He comes and is revealed, we will [as His children] be like Him, because we will see Him just as He is [in all His glory].

August 19

Jesus died for us all. Not just a select few, but all who call Him savior and Lord of their life. Don't keep this wonderful knowledge to yourself but share it with all you meet! Jesus loves us and has redeemed us for his own.

Ephesians 3:14-16

14 For this reason [grasping the greatness of this plan by which Jews and Gentiles are joined together in Christ [I bow my knees [in reverence] before the Father [of our Lord Jesus Christ] 15 from whom every family in heaven and on earth derives its name [God—the first and ultimate Father]. 16 May He grant you out of the riches of His glory, to be strengthened and spiritually energized with power through His Spirit in your inner self, [indwelling your innermost being and personality],

August 20

The world and its charms can be tempting and influence your mind before you realize it. That's why we need to keep our minds rooted in the word of God and take our concerns and fears to Him. The world cannot give us peace; only He can.

Romans 12:2

2 And do not be conformed to this world [any longer with its superficial values and customs], but be transformed and progressively changed [as you mature spiritually] by the renewing of your mind [focusing on godly values and ethical attitudes], so that you may prove [for yourselves] what the will of God is, that which is good and acceptable and perfect [in His plan and purpose for you].

August 21

Satan is the ruler of the world. His "theology" pervades this culture. If you are uncomfortable in society today, rejoice, because, as a child of the living God, you should feel so. Keep your eyes on Him, and know you are just traveling through on the way to your permanent home.

John 15:19

19 If you belonged to the world, the world would love [you as] its own and would treat you with affection. But you are not of the world [you no longer belong to it], but I have chosen you out of the world. And because of this the world hates you.

August 22

The world can be tempting. From the anti-wrinkle cream to must have fashion to sports memorabilia what your team in winning. But Christ reminds us many times that what is treasure here is dust in heaven's regard. Let your eyes linger on the word, and your mind on Christ.

1 John 2:15-17

15 Do not love the world [of sin that opposes God and His precepts], not the things that are in the world. If anyone loves the world, the love of the Father is not in him. 16 For all that is in the world – the list and sensual craving of the flesh and the lust and longing of the eyes and the boastful pride of life [pretentious confidence in one's resources or in the stability of earthly things] – these do not come from the Father, but and from the world. 17 The world is passing away, and with it its lusts [the shameful pursuits and ungodly longings]; but the one who does the will of God and carries out His purposes lives forever.

August 23

Arrogance carries the idea of self-sufficiency; reliance only on one's self, today's culture applauds this attitude. But God says a humble attitude is the beginning of wisdom, the correct approach to learning from God. Be on guard against any hint of arrogance in your life.

Proverbs 1:7

7 The [reverent] fear of the Lord [that is, worshiping Him and regarding Him as truly awesome] is beginning and the preeminent part of knowledge [its starting point and its essence]; But arrogant fools despise [skillful and godly] wisdom and instruction and self-discipline.

August 24

Mark gives us a laundry list of sins that stem from a heart focused on the flesh. We can recognize them and see examples daily. Only God's love and our refusal to lose our focus on Him, can win the battle over our earthly selves. Join hands with Him today.

Mark 7:20-22

20 And He said, "whatever comes from [the heart of] a man, that is what defiles and dishonors him. 21 For from within, [that is] out the heart of men, come base and malevolent thoughts and schemes, acts of sexual immorality, thefts, murders, adulteries, 22 acts of greed and covetousness, wickedness, deceit, unrestrained conduct, envy and jealousy, slander and profanity, arrogance and self-righteousness and foolishness (poor judgment).

August 25

God has a never-ending abundance of grace and forgiveness. He loves you more than anything. Never let guilt or pride come between you and your Father. Confess and run back to His arms.

Isaiah 55:6-7

6 Seek the Lord while He may be found;
Call on Him [for salvation] while He is near.
7 Let the wicked leave (behind) his way
And the unrighteous man his thoughts;
And let him return to the Lord,
And He will have compassion (mercy) on him,
And to our God,
For He will abundantly pardon.

August 26

We trust so much in this world; friends, institutions, political figures, even direct deposit! But nothing we trust on earth is completely able to deliver on that trust. Only God stands firm and unchanging. Deposit your trust where it will earn heavenly interest.

Psalm 118:8

*8 It is better to take refuge in the Lord
Than to trust in man.*

August 27

Part of our Christian duty is to choose and use our words wisely. Let the Spirit fill you and guide you to lift up, encourage, and comfort each other, and to share the wonder of a life in Christ.

Proverbs 17:27

27 He who has knowledge restrains and is careful with his words, and a man of understanding and wisdom has a cool spirit (self-control, and even temper).

August 28

It is not easy or popular to be a Christian these days. Hate speech and condemnation come from every corner. But the God we serve is mightier than those who come against us, no matter how we perceive matters. Let faith be your shield. Stand on the trust.

Jeremiah 17:18

18 Let those who persecute me be shamed, but as for me, protect me from shame; Let them lose courage, but let me be undaunted. Bring on them a day of tragedy and destroy them with double destruction.

August 29

The Creator of the universe is waiting to have a conversation with you. He allows nothing to stand in the way of spending time with you. You are His child, His heir, His shining jewel. Connect with Him now.

Job 33:26

26 "He will pray to God, and He shall be favorable to him, so that he looks at His face with joy; For God restores to man His righteousness [that is, his right standing with God—with its joys]

August 30

In our country, it seems new laws come along every day. Some make sense, and some make us scratch our heads. But God's laws are unchanged and provide guidance and wisdom on living a life of obedience and grace. Let His word guide your life.

Psalm 19:7

7 The law of the Lord is perfect (flawless), restoring and refreshing the soul; The statutes of the Lord are reliable and trustworthy, making wise the simple.

August 31

There is a trend in some churches today, to reinvent the Word of God, to interpret it to adapt to what people want to hear or to what they want approval for. But God's Word does not change. It is the same now, as when first revealed to the chosen authors. Be sensitive to false prophets; cling to the Word as it is.

Psalm 19:8

8 The precepts of the Lord are right, bringing joy to the heart; The commandment of the Lord is pure, enlightening the eyes.

September 1

We cannot physically "find" God or pinpoint His location. But all of creation points to His existence, and the word speaks of His character and nature from earth's beginning to its sure end. Believe in Him, and know of His justice will prevail over men, and the evil they do.

Job 37:23

23 "The Almighty – we cannot find Him; He is exalted in power And He will not do violence to [Nor disregard] justice and abundant righteousness.

September 2

Never let your circumstance overwhelm you. Let them turn you to seek God. He is bigger than they will ever be. He can be trusted to handle them, much better than you can.

Psalm 119:2

2 Blessed and favored by God are those who keep His testimonies, and who [consistently] seek Him and long for Him with all their heart.

September 3

Today belongs to the Lord. Take time to praise Him, and to thank Him for all the blessings you have received. Set aside your care, and just be with Him.

Psalm 5:7-8

7 But as for me, I will enter Your house through the abundance of Your steadfast love and tender mercy; At Your holy temple, I will bow [obediently] in reverence for You.

8 O Lord lead me in Your righteousness because of my enemies; Make Your way straight (direct, right) before me.

September 4

Christ can heal us. It may not be physical, as we desire, but He can heal your heart. We have health issues, relationship problems, and outside stress, but when our hearts are aligned with Him, we can have peace in our storm. Does your heart need healing today?

Mark 5:34

34 Then He said to her, "Daughter, your faith [your personal trust and confidence in Me] has restored you to health; go in peace and be [permanently] healed from your suffering."

September 5

No matter what your miry pit is, whether of your own making, or others' design, God is faithful to rescue you and place your feet on solid ground. Focus on Him, and let the mud and dirt fall away. He will save His Child.

Psalm 40:1-3

1 I waited patiently and expectantly for the Lord; And He inclined me and heard my cry. 2 He brought me up out of a horrible pit [of tumult and of destruction], out of the miry clay, And He set my feet upon a rock, steadying my footsteps and establishing my path.

3 He put a new song in my mouth, a song of praise to our God; Many will see and fear [with great reverence] And will trust confidently in the Lord.

September 6

God promises to be with us at all times. We are not promised an easy way through the world, but His presence gives us peace, hope, guidance, and rest. All that we need to make it through any trial.

Exodus 33:14

14 And the Lord said, "My presence shall go with you, and I will give you rest [by bringing you and the people into the promised land]."

September 7

Contentment is a state of mind foreign to our have-it-all society. Something newer, brighter, or fancier is always tempting us (think cell phones). But, living in Christ should be all we need. He has promised to provide for our needs, and He is faithful to do so. Practice contentment today.

1 Timothy 6:6

6 But godliness actually is a source of great gain when accompanied by contentment [that contentment which comes from a sense of inner confidence based on the sufficiency of God].

September 8

No one is immune from sad or despairing times. We live in a fallen world. What makes a difference is where you place your focus in those times. God can put hope and peace in your heart. When you focus on Him, you remember what He has done for you, and the promises He has made. Lift up your eyes to your future.

Psalm 43:5

5 Why are you in despair, O my soul?
And why are you restless and disturbed within me?
Hope in God and wait expectantly for Him, for I shall again praise Him,
The help of my [sad] countenance and my God.

September 9

I challenge you to live free in Christ today. He broke the chains of bondage, those of legalism and man-made rituals. Live in grace, freely given, and love never-ending.

Romans 8:1-2

1 Therefore there is not no condemnation [no guilty verdict, no punishment] for those who are in Christ Jesus [who believe in Him as personal Lord and Savior]. 2 For the law of the Spirit of life [which is] in Christ Jesus [the law of our new being] has set you free from the law of sin and of death.

September 10

Trust in our earthly lives is based on conditions, requiring proof and ongoing review. But trust in God requires no conditions; His word is true and can be completely believed. Freely trust in God today.

Psalm 20:7

7 Some trust in chariots and some in horses,
But we will remember and trust in the name of the Lord our God.

September 11

When we expectantly open the Word, and wait for the Lord, He will reveal truth hidden in Scripture. How many times have you thought "I never read that before?" Wait on the Lord, and He will continue to feed you.

Isaiah 45:3

"I will give you the treasures of darkness [the hoarded treasures] And the hidden riches of secret places, so that you may know that it is I, The Lord, the God of Israel, who calls you (Cyrus the Great) by your name.

September 12

People only have power over you if you allow them to have it. Surrender to Christ and let His holy power flow through you, strengthening you and keeping your focus on Him and the tasks He has for you. Resist the temptation of man and his plans.

Psalm 27:1

1 The Lord is my light and my salvation ---
Whom shall I fear?
The Lord is the refuge and fortress of my life ---
Whom shall I dread?

September 13

The first thing we should do when we approach the throne is recognize the power and position of the one we address. Too often we rush in and let our pleas and petitions tumble out without thinking to acknowledge God's character. Think about Him, what He's done for you, and how He treasures you. Then reorder your prayers.

Psalm 29:1-2

1 Ascribe to the Lord, O sons of the mighty,
Ascribe to the Lord Glory and strength.
2 Ascribe to the Lord the glory due His name;
Worship the Lord in the beauty and majesty of His holiness [as the creator and source of holiness].

September 14

We become consumed daily with problems, allowing them to dominate our minds and sometimes speech. Those problems become idols in a sense, the objects of our obsession. But God has promised His love and grace, and He is constantly with us. Let those concerns fall away; He will provide.

Psalm 30:5

5 For His anger is but for a moment,
His favor is for a lifetime.
Weeping may endure for a night,
But a shout of joy comes in the morning.

September 15

No one likes trials. We would rather sail through life. But trials can build character and bring us closer to God. When you are next standing in a storm, ask "what quality can this produce in me?", and listen for God.

James 1:2-4

2 Consider it nothing but joy, my brothers and sisters, whenever you fall into various trials. 3 Be assured that the testing of your faith [through experience] produces endurance [leading to spiritual maturity, and inner peace]. 4 And let endurance have its perfect result and do a thorough work, so that you may be perfect and completely developed [in your faith], lacking in nothing.

September 16

God gives us good things, blessings and love. Life gives us stress, problems, and heartache. Life is temporary; God is eternal. Look at perspective and rely on Him.

James 1:17

Every good thing given and every perfect gift is from above; it comes down from the Father of lights [the Creator and sustainer of the heavens], In whom there is no variation [no rising or setting] or shadow cast by His turning [for He is perfect and never changes].

September 17

Tithing is both an honor and a praise. All things are given by Him, and all things can be used by Him in His plans. In giving to the church, we cooperate with Him in large outreach. In giving time, we strengthen our home church, and our faith as we see Him in action. Ask Him how you can participate.

Malachi 3:10

10 Bring all the tithes (the tenth) into the storehouse, so that there may be food in My house, and test Me now in this, "says the Lord of host, "if I will not open for you the windows of heaven and pour out for you [so great] a blessing until there is no more room to receive it.

September 18

Thinking before we speak is a trait that many have not cultivated. Scripture notes its value, and James 3 is devoted to taming the tongue. Ask God to guide your words and make you a witness of kindness and encouragement.

Proverbs 25:11

Like apples of gold in settings of silver
Is a word spoken at the right time.

September 19

When we are daily in the Word, and keeping our hearts turned to Him, we can sense more of what His will is. Our prayers and our desires start to align with Him, and wondrous things happen. Stay focused.

I John 5:14-15

14 This is the [remarkable degree of] confidence which we [as believers are entitled to] have before Him: that is we ask anything according to His will, [that is, consistent with His plan and purpose] He hears us. 15 And if we know [for a fact, as indeed we do] that He hears and listens to us in whatever we ask, we [also] know [with settled and absolute knowledge] that we have [granted to us] the requests which we have ask from Him.

September 20

Today thank God for His blessings, and for your salvation. Thank Him for not giving you what you desire, but giving you what He, out of great love, thinks you deserve. What an awesome, amazing God we serve.

Psalm 103:10-11

10 He has not dealt with us according to our sins [as we deserve], Nor rewarded us [with punishment] according to our wickedness. 11 For as the heavens are high above the earth, So great is His lovingkindness toward those who fear and worship Him [with awe-filled respect and deepest reverence].

September 21

God is in charge. In His Word, He has told us, commanded us, and reminded us "fear not." We do not fear because we know His power, might, and sovereignty. Nations and realms will bow before Him, and evil will tremble. He can handle your cares.

Psalm 113:3-4

*3 From the rising of the sun to its setting
The name of the Lord is to be praised [with awe-inspired reverence].
4 The Lord is high above all nations,
And His glory above the heavens.*

September 22

If you know (and love) Christ, then you know peace. Only He can love and heal you, and give you hope. This world will not satisfy, and possessions will fade away. But His call lasts forever.

John 16:33

33 I have told you these things, so that in Me you may have [perfect] peace. In the world you have tribulation and distress and suffering, but be courageous [be confident, be undaunted, be filled with joy]; I have overcome the world. [My conquest is accomplished, My victory abiding.]

September 23

As you draw ever closer to God, you heart will be shaped by Him. His desires will become your desires, and you will want His will to be done. Pray in Him.

Psalm 37:4

4 Delight yourself in the Lord, And He will give you the desires and petitions of your heart.

September 24

A life lived in the fullness of Christ satisfies every longing you have. Let Him provide the bread of life for you through His Word and be nourished every day.

John 4:34

Jesus said to them, "My food is to do the will of Him who sent Me and to completely finish His work."

September 25

Everyday headlines report acts of violence and horror, disrespect and dissent. For us, we must remember to daily seek our Father, and read His words to remember the promises and future we have through Him. Go to Him.

Psalm 31:1

1 In You, O Lord, I have placed my trust and taken refuge;
Let me never be ashamed; In Your righteousness rescue me.

September 26

God has your times in the palms of His hand and will not let them go. He is your safeguard, rock, and fortress. Never doubt Him, even in the worst of times. He has it.

Psalm 31:14-16

14 But as for me, I trust [confidently] in You and Your greatness, O Lord; I said, "You are my God."
15 My times are in Your hands;
Rescue me from the hand of my enemies and from those who pursue and persecute me.
16 Make Your face shine upon Your servant;
Save me in Your lovingkindness.

September 27

At times it is hard to believe that all your sins are forgiven. I mean doesn't God know who you really are? Yes, He does, and He loves you in spite of yourself. Thank Him, and praise Him, and relax in knowing you are covered in the blood.

Psalm 32:1-2

1 Blessed [fortunate, prosperous, favored by God] Is he whose transgression is forgiven, and whose sin is covered.

2 Blessed in the man to whom the Lord does not impute wickedness, and in whose spirit, there is no deceit.

September 28

God has granted you strong roots and has given you gifts to produce fruit for blessings. Relax into Him and let the Spirit guide and flow throughout your life.

Jeremiah 17:7-8

7 "Blessed [with spiritual security] is the man who believes and relies on the Lord And whose hope and confident expectation is the Lord.

8 "For he will be [nourished] like a tree plants by the waters, that spreads out its roots by the river; And will not fear the heat what it domes; But its leaves will be green and moist.

And it will not be anxious and concerned in a year of drought nor stop bearing fruit.

September 29

Even though it appears Satan is winning in this world, the Word tells us the end of the story. We are already victorious through Christ's sacrifice and ultimately, His conquering death, the end result of Sin. Live as the Redeemer's Child!

1 John 4:4

4 Little children (believers, dear ones), you are of God and you belong to Him and have [already] overcome them [the agents of the antichrist]; because He who is in you is greater than he (Satan) who is in the world [of sinful mankind].

September 30

God doesn't intend for you to disappear. God doesn't intend for you to hide or hold back. God is light, and you reflect that to the world. Shine on, God's blessings!

2 Samuel 22:20

20 "He also brought me out to an open place; He rescued me because He delighted in me.

October 1

You are an heir to a tremendous fortune, and a breathtaking mansion. You are rich beyond belief, as a child of the living, eternal, omnipotent God. Live like this, thanking Him at all times for His grace.

Colossians 1:12

12 Giving thanks to the Father, who has qualified us to share in the inheritance of the saints (God's people) in the Light.

October 2

The world looks at wisdom in many different ways; financial wizards, creative geniuses, electronic gurus. But true wisdom comes from knowing God, and His Word. When we are thus equipped, we can discern truth from lies, correct choices from wrong temptations, and real worth from cheap invitations. Study to become wise.

Proverbs 1:33

33 "But whoever listens to me (Wisdom) will live securely and in confident trust and will be at ease, without fear or dread of evil."

October 3

When we feel threatened, overwhelmed, or frightened, we can seek shelter in our God. He never forsakes us, but stands all-powerful, ready to comfort and to fight for His child. Run to Him today.

Psalm 57:1

1 Be gracious to me, O God, be gracious and merciful to me, for my soul finds shelter and safety in You, and in the shadow of Your wings I will take refuge and be confidently secure Until destruction passes by.

October 4

You are never too far away from God to call to Him. He holds you tight even when you push Him away. Yield to Him, and rest in His arms.

Psalm 61:2-3

2 From the end of the earth I call to You, when my heart is overwhelmed and weak; Lead me to the Rock the is higher than I [a rock the is too high to reach without Your help].

October 5

Waiting is very hard. We like to move on, staying in a state of perpetual motion. But God tells us to be still and wait on Him. Indeed, that is one of the best ways to hear His voice. Seek a quiet place today, and spend some time waiting on God.

Psalm 62:5-7

5 For God alone my soul waits in silence and quietly submits to Him, for my hope is from Him.

6 He only is my rock and my salvation; My fortress and my defense, I will not be shaken or discouraged.

7 On God my salvation and my glory rest; He is my rock of [unyielding] strength, my refuge is in God.

October 6

You know your own faults, regrets, and secret sins, and most of the time, you beat yourself up over them. But, through the eyes of God, you are a shining, sinless, perfect creature, washed clean with the blood of the Lamb. Live in that knowledge today.

Jude 1:24-25

24 Now to Him who is able to keep you from stumbling or falling into sin, and to present you unblemished [blameless and faultless] in the presence of His glory with triumphant joy and unspeakable delight,

25 to the only God our Savior, through Jesus Christ our Lord, be glory, majesty, dominion, and power, before all time and now and forever. Amen.

October 7

Look at your left hand. Squeeze it like you are holding another hand, now, realize that you are holding God's hand. He has promised that to you. You are never alone.

Psalm 73:23-24

23 Nevertheless I am continually with You; You have taken hold of my right hand.

24 You will guide me with Your counsel, and afterward receive me to honor and glory.

October 8

Jesus is everything you need. Nothing on the earth satisfies like a relationship with Him. Stay connected to Him, and live and life of freedom through Him.

Psalm 73:25-26

25 Whom have I in heaven [but You]? And besides You, I desire nothing on earth.

26 My flesh and my heart may fail, But God is the rock and strength of my heart and my portion forever.

October 9

God knows everything about you, everything that would happen to you, and the outcome of your trials thousands of years before you were born. Your life can be trusted to Him, because He loves you, plans for you, and you matter to Him. Thank Him that your steps are ordered by Him.

Psalm 31:15

15 My times are in Your hands; Rescue me from the hand of my enemies and from those who pursue and persecute me.

October 10

Never pass up a chance to be kind or to show mercy. You are not glorifying yourself, but you are growing in the image of Christ. Study His character and ask the Father to mold you in His likeness.

Proverbs 3:3

3 Do not let mercy and kindness and truth leave you [instead let these qualities define you]; Bind them [securely] around your neck, Write them on the tablet of your heart.

October 11

What a glorious future awaits us in heaven! Nothing you have done for God will go unappreciated. No awards, accolades, or honors here on earth will compare to the crown and robe He has prepared for you. Keep looking up.

Matthew 20:16

16 So those who are last [in this world] shall be first [in the world to come], and those who are first, last.

October 12

Every job has dignity, even though culture seems to have a standard of worth for positions. A Christian realizes God has placed them in their particular workplace for a reason and does his or her job to the best of their individual ability to praise God, not man. Remember to whom we own honor.

Colossians 3:23-24

23 Whatever you do [whatever your task may be], work from the soul [that is, put in your very best effort], as [something done] for the Lord and not for men, 24 Knowing [with all certainty] that it is from the Lord [not from men] that you will receive the inheritance which is your [greatest] reward. It is the Lord Christ whom you [actually] serve.

October 13

God has given you a special talent to share with the world. He said so, and you can believe Him. Ask Him to show you your talent, and how He wishes you to use it in service to Him. He wants His special child to shine.

1 Peter 4:10

10 Just as each one of you has received a special gift [a spiritual talent, and ability graciously given by God], employ it in serving one another as [is appropriate for] good stewards of God's multi-faceted grace [faithfully using the diverse, varied gifts and abilities granted to Christians by God's unmerited favor].

October 14

God always satisfies our longing… for love, for companionship, for guidance, for comfort. There is no emotional or physical state that He cannot handle. He created us and knows us better than anyone. Keep Him close.

Psalm 42:1-2

1 As the deer pants [longingly] for the water books, So my soul pants [longingly] for You, O God.

2 My soul (my life, my inner self) thirsts for God, for the living God. When will I come, and see the face of God?

October 15

May the Lord fill your heart with love, washing away any hurts, bitterness, and selfishness that may be there. Let Him guide you in loving others as He loves us. Honor the Sabbath with Your hearts.

1 Thessalonians 3:11-13

11 Now may our God and Father Himself, and Jesus our Lord guise our steps to you [by removing the obstacles that stand in our way]. 12 And may the Lord cause you to increase and excel and overflow in love for one another, and for all people, just as we also do for you; 13 so the He may strengthen and establish your hearts without blame in holiness in the sight of our God and Father at the coming of our Lord Jesus with all His saints (God's people).

October 16

We can depend on nothing in this world; not money, possessions, or people, no matter how close to us they are. But God is unchanging, and rock holding strong in the storms we experience. Hold fast to Him, giving your love and trust to Him.

Psalm 61:1-2

1 Hear my cry, O God; Listen to my prayer.

2 From the end of the earth I call to You, when my heart is overwhelmed and weak; Lead me to the rock that is higher than I [a rock that is too high to reach without Your help].

October 17

The word is full of wisdom, for daily life, for future planning, and for relationships. The world offers wisdom, but only from a present-day perspective. Look for eternal wisdom.

Philippians 4:6-7

6 Do not be anxious or worried about anything, but in everything [every circumstance and situation] by prayer and petition with thanksgiving, continues to make your [specific] requests known to God. 7 And the peace of God [that peace which] stands guard over your hearts and your minds in Christ Jesus [is yours].

October 18

At times, we try to put human attributes on God, such as our ideas of punishment, and conditional love. Our God doesn't work like us; He is full of mercy, grace, and love. He has promised His love to His children, poured out like water all over us. Thank Him today.

Psalm 84:11

11 For the Lord God is a sun and shield; The Lord bestows grace and favor and honor; No good thing will He withhold from those who walk uprightly.

October 19

The Lord is good. While things may happen in our lives that we don't understand, and may cause us to doubt His plan, He remains steadfast in His goodness. Remember, Satan is the initiator of doubt; God works for good in the lives of those who love Him.

Psalm 85:9-12

9 Surely His salvation is near to those who [reverently] fear Him [and obey Him with submissive wonder], That glory [the manifest presence of God] may dwell in our land.

10 Steadfast love and truth and faithfulness meet together; Righteousness and peace kiss each other.

11 Truth springs from the earth, and righteousness looks down from heaven.

12 Indeed, the Lord will give what is good, and our land will yield its produce.

October 20

God is longing to talk to you, and to shower you with blessings. He loves you and wants to guide and to protect you. Spend some time with Him today.

Psalm 86:5,15

5 For You, O Lord, are good, and ready to forgive [our sins, sending them away, completely letting them go forever and ever]; And

abundantly in lovingkindness and overflowing in mercy to all those who call upon You.

15 But You, O Lord, are a God [who protects and is] merciful and gracious, Slow to anger and abounding in lovingkindness and truth.

October 21

The Word tells us over and over that God is faithful and can be trusted to protect and to love us. Establish Him as your safe place, and never fear what man desires again.

Psalm 46:1

God is our refuge and strength [mighty and impenetrable], A very present and well-proved help in trouble.

October 22

Waiting on the Lord and His response can be hard, but we know the answer will be worth the time spent waiting. Wait with confidence and trust.

Psalm 27:14

14 Wait for and confidently expect the Lord; Be strong and let your heart take courage; Yes, wait for and confidently expect the Lord.

October 23

Security is not found in a job position, possessions, friends, or politics. Security is found in loving, trusting, and obeying God, our eternal Father. Set your sights above.

Psalms 91:1-2

1 He who dwells in the shelter of the Most High Will remain secure and rest in the shadow of the Almighty [whose power no enemy can withstand].

2 I will say of the Lord, "He is my refuge and my fortress, My God, in whom I trust [with great confidence, and on whom I rely]!"

October 24

In times of stress, a comforting thing to do is to look back, and see how God's hand has shaped and worked in our lives. In doing so, we reassure ourselves that He is at work in the present time too. He is a faithful God.

Psalm 77:11

I will [solemnly] remember the deeds of the Lord; Yes, I will [wholeheartedly] remember Your wonders of old.

October 25

God gives you enough grace everyday especially for that day. He is with you every step, and paves that way through trials and obstacles you face. Do not concern yourself with tomorrow; you will have fresh grace poured over that day.

2 Corinthians 12:9

9 but He has said to me, "My grace is sufficient for you [My lovingkindness and My mercy are more than enough—always available—regardless of the situation]; for [My] power is being perfected [and is completed and shows itself most effectively] in [your] weakness." Therefore, I will all the more gladly boast in my weaknesses, so that the power of Christ [may completely enfold me and] may dwell in me.

October 26

One of God's most loving characteristics is His refusal to bring up your past sins. He erases them, blots them out, casts them into the sea, how wonderful! If He can do that, we can find the strength to forgive ourselves and others.

Zephaniah 3:17

17 "The Lord your God is in your midst, A Warrior who saves. He will rejoice over you with joy; He will be quiet in His love [making no mention of your past sins], He will rejoice over you with shouts of joy.

October 27

Although never pleasant, trials provide a way to grow and to strengthen our faith. Perspective has a lot to do with how we endure these trials. If we can concentrate on the fact that we will come out of our circumstances clean to God, and with more understanding of His plans and power, we can walk confidently through the fire holding tightly to His hand.

James 1:3

3 Be assured that the testing of your faith [through experience] produces endurance [leading to spiritual maturity, and inner peace].

October 28

When you feel low or discouraged, remember that God is holding His arms out to pick you up, just as an earthly father picks up his toddler learning to walk. Maybe that is how He see us through His loving eyes; His toddler learning to walk in His ways. Let Him lift you up.

Psalm 116:5-6

5 Gracious is the Lord, and [consistently] righteous; Yes, our God is compassionate.

6 The Lord protects the simple (childlike); I was brought low [humbled and discouraged], and He saved me.

October 29

Praising God in the midst of trials has the effect of lifting your spirit, lessening worries, and refocusing your heart on Him. Lift you voice to Him on the Lord's day.

Psalm 117

1 O Praise the Lord, all you nations! Praise Him, all you people!

2 For His lovingkindness prevails over us [and we triumph and overcome through Him], And the truth of the Lord endures forever. Praise the Lord! (Hallelujah)

October 30

No matter how much we love or trust someone, it is a human fact that sooner or later they will disappoint us. The same is not true of God. He is faithful; His nature will not let Him be otherwise. Put your trust in Him, and you will experience true reliance.

Psalm 118:8-9

8 It is better to take refuge in the Lord Than to trust in man.

9 It is better to take refuge in the Lord Than to trust in princes.

October 31

Everything in the world in temporary. Amassing wealth and possessions may be status in the world's eyes but will not bring peace or eternal life as God can. Establish your life in Him and gain true prosperity.

Psalm 127:1

1 Unless the Lord builds the house,
They labor in vain who build it;
Unless the Lord guards the city,
The watchman keeps awake in vain.

November 1

Today's Scripture comes from a psalm of ascent, a song sung by pilgrims as they climbed to Jerusalem. We can sing it as we climb toward our goal of eternal life with Jesus in the heavenly home He has waiting for us. What a glorious vision!

Psalm 128:1

1 Blessed [happy and sheltered by God's favor] is everyone who fears the Lord worships Him with obedience], Who walks in His ways and lives according to His commandments.

November 2

When your heart is heavy, look to God. He has promised to put a new heart in you, to lift you up, and make you like new creation. He is faithful, and His love is boundless. Let Him do His work in you.

Ezekiel 36:25-26

25 Then I will sprinkle clean water on you, and you will be clean; I will cleanse you from all your uncleanness and from all your idols. 26 Moreover, I will give you a new heart and put a new spirit within you, and I will remover the heart of stone from you flesh and give you a heart of flesh.

November 3

God forgives us of our sins. A simple statement but so powerful. Men keep tabs on slights and resentments, but God gives us grace even when we don't deserve it. Thank Him today, and live free in His love.

Psalm 130:3-4

3 If You, Lord, should keep an account of our sins and treat us accordingly, O Lord, who could stand [before You in judgement and claim innocence]?

4 But there is forgiveness with You, That You may be feared and worshiped [with submissive wonder].

November 4

The first thing to remember about praying is our prayers must be in line with God's will. It's not all about "me." We can present desires and concerns, but with an obedient heart that understands God may not answer exactly as we ask. We can trust His plan is perfect, even when we can't see the end yet.

Mark 11:24

24 For this reason I am telling you, whatever things you ask for in prayer [in accordance with God's will], believe [with confident trust] that you have received them, and they will be given to you.

November 5

God desires that we live in unity with our Christian family. We don't always agree, but we should never use disagreement as an excuse to gossip or disrespect our brethren. Be loyal to God and His church.

Psalm 133:1

1 Behold, how good and how pleasant it is for brothers to dwell together in unity!

November 6

God is good. He desires a relationship with you and covets your love. He even provided a costly way for your salvation. Don't run from Him or be afraid to approach Him when you feel guilty. His love and goodness will always be there for His children.

Psalm 115:14-15

14 May the Lord give you [great] increase, You and your children.

15 May you be blessed of the Lord, Who made heaven and earth.

November 7

At times, we are so caught up in this present life that we forget this existence is not all there is. In fact, what happens on earth is almost the polar opposite of what our eternal life will be. Praise God for giving us a glimpse of the "rest of the story"

Revelations 21:1-5

1 Then I saw a new heaven and a new earth; for the first heaven and the first earth had passed away (vanished), and there is no longer and sea. 2 And I saw the holy city, new Jerusalem, coming down out of heaven from God, arrayed like a bride adorned for her husband; 3 and then I heard a loud voice from the throne, saying, "See! The tabernacle of God is among men, and He will live among them, and they will be His people, and God Himself will be with them [as their God,] 4 and He will wipe away every tear from their eyes; and there will no longer be death; there will no longer be sorrow and anguish, or crying, or pain; for the former order of things has passed away."

5 And He who sits on the throne said, "Behold, I am making all things new." Also, He said, "Write, for these words are faithful and true [they are accurate, incorruptible, and trustworthy]."

November 8

In this time of sorrow and brokenness, we often feel the presence of God the most. We run to His arms, seeking strength, comfort, and healing. He is just as accessible in the time of peace too. He loves you at all times.

Psalm 34:18

18 The Lord is near to the heartbroken And He saves those who are crushed in spirit (contrite in heart, truly sorry for their sin).

November 9

As we trust God's love and care, we can trust that sadness lasts only for a time. Jesus taught that true joy comes from abiding in Him. With that knowledge, we can press through circumstances knowing our peace is secure with Jesus.

Psalm 30:5

5 For His anger is but for a moment,
His favor is for a lifetime.
Weeping may endure for a night,
But a shout of joy comes in the morning.

November 10

Children are held in high esteem by God. Jesus loved to be surrounded by little ones. Today, many people do not cherish their children, or give them love and support. Remember that we are all God's children and extend love to the kids that come in your world. You may be the adult they need.

Proverbs 3:22

22 And they will be life to your soul (your inner self) And a gracious adornment to your neck (your outer self).

November 11

How would you change your daily routine if you imagined yourself as a letter from Christ to the world? We are just that, as Scripture tells us over and over that we are not of the world but set apart. Our lives are testimonies, demonstrating what a Christian is. What will your letter say today?

2 Corinthians 3:3

3 You show that you are a letter from Christ, delivered by us, written not with ink but with the Spirit of the living God, not on tablets of stone but on tablets of human hearts.

November 12

As we get older, we feel the wear and tear on our earthly vessels. God has promised His care and provision in those times, even promising to carry us. He has promises for every life stage, we experience. What a loving Father we serve.

Isaiah 46:4

4 Even to your old age I am He,
And even to your advanced old age I will carry you!
I have made you, and I will carry you;
Be assured I will carry you and I will save you.

November 13

Our guide book for navigating this world is the Word of God. The world is sneaky; it can infiltrate our minds and behavior, and before we know it, we are indistinguishable from everyone else. Ask God every day to show you where you may be harming your walk and hold every thought and behavior up against the Word and let God shape you in His image.

Romans 12:2

2 And do not be conformed to this world [any longer with its superficial values and customs], but be transformed and progressively changed [as you mature spiritually] by the renewing of your mind [focusing on godly values and ethical attitudes], so that you may prove [for yourselves what the will of God is, that which is good and acceptable and perfect [in His plan and purpose for you].

November 14

It is difficult for Christians these days. We face criticism, censure, and even persecution. Churches are not necessarily safe havens anymore. But, living for Christ will bring its own rewards, more then we can imagine or envision. Live in a way that you will stand blameless on the day of judgement.

1 Peter 4:17-19

17 For it is the time [destined] for judgment to begin with the household of God; and it begins with us, what will the outcome be for those who do not respect or believe or obey the gospel of God? 18 And if it is difficult for the righteous to be saved, what will become of the godless and the sinner? 19 Therefore, those who are ill-treated and suffer in accordance with the will of God must [continue to] do right and commit their souls [for safe-keeping] to the faithful Creator.

November 15

God is all knowing and perceives our every thought. But He wants us to talk to Him, and share our hearts and desires with Him, so He can grant us that which is good and in His plan for us. He works to conform us to the image of His son, but we need to dialogue with Him to accomplish this. Have a little talk with Jesus today.

Philippians 4:6-7

6 Do not be anxious or worried about anything, but in everything [every circumstance and situation] by prayer and petition with thanksgiving, continue to make your [specific requests know to God. 7 And the peace of God [that peace which reassures the heart, that peace] which transcends all understanding, [that peace which] stands guard over your hearts and your minds in Christ Jesus [is yours].

November 16

Praising God refocuses our attention on Him and allows the troubles we have to fall away in the face of acknowledging His power and goodness. Thank Him now and take some time to meditate on His character.

Psalm 32:11

11 Be glad in the Lord and rejoice, you righteous [who actively seek right sanding with Him]; Shout for joy, all you upright in heart.

November 17

God never tells us to fear. Rather, we are told repeatedly "do not fear". Read Joshua 1. We have a Father that will fight for us, walk beside us, and guides us daily. He wants us to depend on Him totally. Do that today, walk by faith.

Isaiah 41:10

10 `Do not fear [anything], for I am your God.
Do not be afraid, for I am your God.
I will strengthen you, be assured I will help you;
I will certainly take hold of you with My righteous right hand [a hand of justice, of power, of victory, of salvation].'

November 18

God not only tells us not to fear, but commands us not to fear. He is the all-powerful God, creator of the earth and heavens. We can put our faith in Him to care for us.

Joshua 1:9

9 Have I not commanded you? Be strong and courageous! Do not be terrified or dismayed (intimidated), for the Lord your God is with you wherever you go?

November 19

Scripture in full of proof that God is faithful, both to provide for our needs, and to provide sanctuary and protection. Trust Him with your life today and turn your problems over to him.

Psalm 46:1

1 God is our refuge and strength [mighty and impenetrable], A very present and well-proved help in trouble.

November 20

Truly everything we have is a blessing from God. We don't own anything; everything, to the cows on a thousand hills, is His. Refuse to hold tight to possessions, and instead, hold fast to His hand, and trust He will provide.

Job 1:20-21

20 Then job got up and tore his robe and shaved his head [in mourning for the children], and he fell to the ground and worshiped [God].

21 He said, "Naked (without possessions) I came [into this world] from my mother's womb, and naked I will return there. The Lord gave and the Lord has taken away; Blessed be the name of the Lord.

November 21

Keep your eyes focused upwards. God is sovereign and His throne is in the heavens. He is the ruler of all, and He is your Father. Let Him handle your troubles.

Psalm 121:1-2

*1 I will lift up my eyes to the hills [of Jerusalem] ---
From where shall my help come?
2 My help comes from the Lord,
Who made heaven and earth.*

November 22

Sometimes we feel God is faraway. In truth, we are the ones who moved. Maybe little sins have crept in that makes us feel guilty, or maybe life has crowded in, keeping us too busy. Run back to Him today! He's waiting with open arms.

Malachi 3:7

7 "Yet from the days of your fathers you have turned away from My statutes and ordinances and have not kept them. Return to Me, and I will return to you," say the Lord of hosts. "But you say, `how shall we return?'

November 23

On this day of thanksgiving, remember all good gifts come from God the Father. He loves His children and desires a close relationship with you. Adopt an attitude of gratitude.

Psalm 62:5

5 For God alone my should waits in silence and quietly submits to Him, for my hope is from Him.

November 24

God listens to every word of our conversations with Him. His response may not come according to our timeline, but He has made note of your requests, and is seeing if they line up with His plan for you. Be patient, read the word, and ask Him to continue shaping you in Christ's image. The answer will come.

1 John 5:14-15

14 This is the [remarkable degree of] confidence which we [as believers are entitled to] have before Him: that is, we ask anything according to His will, [that is consistent with His plan and purpose] He hears us. 15 And is we know [for a fact, as indeed we do] that He hears and listens to us in whatever we ask, we [also] know [with settled and absolute knowledge] that we have [granted to us] the requests which we have asked from Him.

November 25

Discipline yourself to act out of love. Love is the example Christ gave us and living in love aids us conforming us to His image. Dine freely of the grace that has been given to you.

Ephesians 4:15

15 But speaking the truth in love [in all things—both our speech and our lives expressing His truth], let us grow up in all things into Him [following His example] who is the Head---Christ.

November 26

When we love the Lord, obedience is not a burden, it is an act of love. We understand that the Father gives us commands and percepts for our protection and blessings. Give Him thanks for providing the Word to guide us in all we do.

1 Samuel 15:22

22 Samuel said, "Has the Lord as great a delight in burnt offerings and sacrifices as in obedience to the voice of the Lord?

Behold, to obey is better than sacrifice, and to heed [is better] than the fat of rams.

November 27

Scripture contains not only God's commands, percepts, and guidance, but also example after example of His Word being proven true and unchanging. When doubts assail your mind, go to the Word. You can rest on that foundation.

Proverbs 30:5

5 Every word of God is tested and refined [like silver]; He is a shield to those who trust and take refuge in Him.

November 28

Trials have the ability to cause us to lose our focus, to let out hearts and eyes stray from God. When you find that happening, stop, refocus, and stay in the word. Let trials bring you closer to God.

James 1:12

12 Blessed [happy, spiritually prosperous, favored by God] is the man who is steadfast under trial and perseveres when tempted; for when he has passed the test and been approved, he will receive the [victor's] crown of life which the Lord has promised to those who love Him.

November 29

We humans have the desire to form God into a being that matches us, in thought and character. But the truth is there are no human images or descriptions that can describe the might, the power, and the thoughts of God. Worship Him for His majesty, and rest in the Word, which tells us all we need to know about Him.

Exodus 3:14

14 God said to Moses, "I Am Who I Am"; and HE said, "You shall say this to the Israelites, 1I Am has sent me to you."

November 30

When God desired to grant Solomon the desire of his heart, Solomon asked for wisdom. Wisdom doesn't come quickly but is achieved through discipline and study. Ask God for wisdom today and begin with the scripture.

Psalm 119:34

34 Give me understanding [a teachable heart and the ability to learn], that I may keep Your law; And observe it with all my heart.

December 1

When you fully trust the Lord, He works within you to open your heart and eyes to the riches that He provides for you. The world may define wealth a different way, but nothing compares to the abundance of life as a child of the King.

Isaiah 45:3

3 "I will give you the treasures of darkness [the hoarded treasures] And the hidden riches of secret places, so that you may know that it is I, The Lord, the God of Israel, who calls you (Cyrus the Great) by your name.

December 2

Leading others to Christ is the biggest gift you can give anyone. Be filled with the excitement and love that Christmas brings, and remember the reason for the season.

Daniel 12:3

3 Those who are [spiritually] wise will shine brightly like the brightness of the expanse of heaven, and those who lead many to the righteousness, [will shine] like the stars forever and ever.

December 3

Scripture is unchanging, as true today as it was centuries ago. It can guide you in making decisions, fill you with confidence, make you wise, and grow your relationship with God. Spend time daily in the Word.

Romans 15:4

4 For whatever was written in earlier times was written for our instruction, so that through endurance and the encouragement of the Scriptures we might have hope and overflow with confidence in His promises.

December 4

Our present and future is grounded in Christ, everything in this world is temporary, but Christ is eternal. Our faith and hope reside in Him. Depend only on Him.

John 6:68

Simon Peter answered, "Lord, to whom shall we go? You [alone] have the words of eternal life [you are our only hope].

December 5

Being a Christ follower means you desire Him above all else, seeing everything the world offers as dust in comparison. In this season, where materialism is foremost, examine your heart and see if He really sits on the throne.

Philippians 3:7

7 But whatever former things were gains to me [as I thought then], these things [once regarded as advancement in merit] I have come to consider as loss [absolutely worthless] for the sake of Christ [and the purpose which He has given my life].

December 6

Today's scripture, from Zachariah, refers to seven eyes. This refers to God's oversight of the world and its inhabitants. Another way to look at it is God's watchful care of His children. It also references His delight in the beginning of the building to His temple. He is no less delighted when you give your life to be His temple. Thank Him for keeping His eyes on you at all times, and rest in His care. Honor Him with your life.

Zachariah 4:10

10 Who [with reason] despises the day of small things (beginnings)? For these seven [eyes] shall rejoice when they see the plumb line in the hand of Zerubbabel. They are the eyes of the Lord which roams throughout the earth.

December 7

Our human inclination is pride; when we accomplish something, we want accolades, praise. But God loves a humble attitude, because our spiritual gifts are given by Him, for honoring Him, and serving Him. Do a checklist mentally today on pride; don't get "too big for your britches"

1 Peter 5:5

5 Likewise, you younger men [of lesser rank and experience], be subject to your elders [seek their counsel]; and all of you, clothe yourselves with humility toward one another [tie on the servant's apron], for God is opposed to the proud [the disdainful, the presumptuous, and He defeats them], but He gives grace to the Humble.

December 8

You have been redeemed by God from sin and Satan. His Son shed His blood to cover your sins, and insure eternal life for you, to spend it in Heaven in the home prepared for you there. Let this knowledge lift your heart and fill you with praise.

Psalm 34:22

22 The Lord redeems the soul of His servants, and none of those who take refuge in Him will be condemned.

December 9

We have knowledge that through our faith in Jesus, we have escaped eternal punishment. Let that truth spur you into action, letting others know about the hope Jesus gives. Be a witness for God's love.

Hebrews 10:30-31

30 For we know Him who said, "Vengeance is Mine [retribution and deliverance of justice rest in ME], I will repay [the wrongdoer]." And again, "The Lord will judge His people". 31 It is a fearful and terrifying thing to fall into the hands of the living God [incurring His judgement and wrath].

December 10

Glory in God today! Throw yourself into worshiping Him this Sabbath, and into delighting yourself in His plan for you. Come Lord Jesus, come!

Psalm 37:4-6

4 Delight yourself in the Lord, And He will give you the desires and petitions of your heart.

5 Commit your way to the Lord; Trust in Him also and He will do it.

6 He will make your righteousness [your pursuit of right standing with God] like the light,

And your judgment like [the shining of] the noonday [sun].

December 11

When we were called by Christ, we probably assumed we would be serving; after all, isn't that what Christians do? But, we are also called to be thankful, living with gratitude at all times for what God is, and will be, doing for us. Live gratefully today.

2 Thessalonians 2:13-17

13 But we should and are [morally] obligated [as debtors] always to give thanks to God for you, believers beloved by the Lord, because God has chosen you from the beginning for salvation through the sanctifying work of the Spirit [that sets you apart for God's purpose] and by your faith in the truth [of God's work that leads you to spiritual maturity]. 14 It was to this end that He called you through our gospel [the good news of Jesus' death, burial, and resurrection], so that you may obtain and share in the glory of our Lord Jesus Christ. 15 So then, brother and sisters, stand firm and hold [tightly] to the traditions which you were taught, whether by word of mouth or by letter from us.

16 Now may our Lord Jesus Christ Himself and God our Father, who has loved us and given us everlasting comfort and encouragement and the good [well-founded] hope [of salvation] by His grace, 17 comfort and encourage and strengthen your hearts [keeping them steadfast and on course] in every good work and word.

December 12

"Redeemed" essentially means "to buy back", or "to rescue". God redeemed you with the blood of His own Son. Do you realize how precious you are to Him? You are a diamond in His eyes. Carry that knowledge inside you today and carry yourself like the blessing you are.

Psalm 34:22

22 The Lord redeems the soul of His servants, and none of those who take refuge in Him will be condemned.

December 13

Soak in God's greatness today. Reflect on the times in the past He has brought you through, and the little blessings He sends every day. He loves it when His children thank Him for those blessings. Praise Him today.

Psalm 145:9

9 The Lord is good to all, And His tender mercies are over all His works [the entirety of things created].

December 14

If we are to model ourselves after Christ, we must be good to everyone. Christ played no favorites, and neither should we. Show the same kindness and attention to those you meet on the street as to those you worship with each Sabbath. Be love and light, even as Christ.

Galatians 6:10

So then, while we (as individual believers) have the opportunity, let us do good to all people (not only being helpful, but also doing that which promotes their spiritual well-being), and especially (be a blessing) to those of the household of faith (born-again believers).

December 15

God blesses a life of faith. Stepping out in trust can be scary, but knowing God is holding your hand, smiling at your obedience, makes it all worthwhile. We can't imagine what He has in store for us.

John 20:29

29 Jesus said to him, "Because you have seen Me, do you now believe? Blessed [happy, spiritually secure, and favored by God] are they who did not see [Me] and yet believed [in Me].

December 16

In our very judgmental society, mercy is a quality often spurned. But, without God's great mercy, we would not have a savior, and the promises of eternal life with Him in our forever home. Stop yourself the next time a negative attitude enters your mind and see if mercy is warranted.

Ephesians 2:4-5

4 But God, being [so very] rich in mercy, because of His great and wonderful love with which He loved us, 5 even when we were [spiritually] dead and separated from Him because of our sins, He made us [spiritually] alive together with Christ (for by His grace – His undeserved favor and mercy --- you have been saved from God's judgement).

December 17

Jesus' sacrifice not only brought a way to reconciliation with God but opened the Good News to Gentiles the non-Jewish people. Thank God for this wonderful gift, the baby we celebrate this season.

Ephesians 2:15-16

15 by abolishing in His [own crucified] flesh the hostility caused by the Law with its commandments contained in ordinances [which He satisfied]; so that in Himself He might make the two into one new man, thereby establishing peace. 16 And [that He] might reconcile them both [Jew and Gentile, united] in one body to God through the cross, thereby putting to death the hostility.

December 18

If we are not grounded, we can be flighty, prone to spur-of-the-moment decisions, and opinions shaped by whoever happens to be around at the moment. Let yourself be grounded in God, His Word, and His communion with you in prayer. Know your worth in Him and stay true to that.

Isaiah 7:9b

9b If you will not believe [and trust in God and His message], be assured that you will not be established.

December 19

If you listen to the "wise" people of today, you will certainly be anxious, fearful, and worried. But God commands us to separate, and fear nothing, and trust no one but Him. Live a victorious life through His leading; rise above!

Isaiah 8:11-13

11 For in this way the Lord spoke to me with His strong hand [upon me] and instructed me not to walk in the way of this people [behaving as they do], saying, 12 "You are not to say, `It is a conspiracy!'

In regard to all that this people call a conspiracy, and you are not to fear what they fear nor be in dread of it.

13 "It is the Lord of hosts whom you are to regard as holy and awesome. He shall be your [source of] fear, He shall be your [source of] dread [not man].

December 20

Make it a practice to watch for God in your day. Don't expect huge appearances but look for the little blessings that He so generously gives. He works tirelessly in your day. Thank Him.

Isaiah 8:17

17 And I will wait for the Lord who is hiding His face from the house of Jacob; and I will look eagerly for Him.

December 21

We are on the verge of celebrating the gift of God's illumination to the lost world! Jesus truly is the light of the world: He is the Light of your life. Even in the soul's dark times, He makes love and truth shine through. Praise Him today.

Isaiah 9:2

The people who walk in (spiritual) darkness will see a great Light; Those who live in the dark land, The Light will shine on them.

December 22

Jesus is many things to each of us, Savior, friend, instructor. But perhaps Isaiah portrayed Him best in the prophecy given so many, many years earlier. Meditate on each of these titles and reflect on how Jesus meets that need in your life.

Isaiah 9:6

*6 For to us a Child as be born, to us a Son shall be given;
And the government shall be upon His shoulder,
And His name shall be called Wonderful Counselor, Mighty God, Everlasting Father, Prince of Peace.*

December 23

The same spirit that rested on Jesus is promised to dwell within a believer when He accepts Christ as Savior. You are the home of the Spirit; listen to Him. Conduct yourself as a tabernacle for God. Worship continually.

Isaiah 11:2-3

2 And the Spirit of the Lord will rest on Him ---
The Spirit of counsel and strength,
The Spirit of knowledge and of the [reverential and obedient] fear of the Lord ---

3 And He will delight in the fear of the Lord,
And He will not judge by what His eyes see,
Nor make decisions be what His ears hear;

December 24

The Word of God has the power to change you, guide you, and form you into Christ's image if you let it. Remember always, the Word is God speaking to you. Listen.

1 Thessalonians 2:13

13 And we also thank God continually for this, that when you received the word of God [concerning salvation] which you heard from us, you welcomed it not as the word of [mere] men, but as it truly is, the word of God, which is effectually at work in you who believe [exercising its inherent, supernatural power in those of faith].

December 25

Today, remember the best gift you, and the world ever received. Don't lose sight of why Christmas is a sacred, holy observance.

Luke 2:6-20

6 While they were there [in Bethlehem], the time came for her to give birth, 7 and she gave birth to her Son, her firstborn; and she wrapped Him in [swaddling] cloths and laid Him in a manger, because there was no [private] room for them in the inn.

8 In the same region there were shepherds staying out in the fields, keeping watch over their flock by night. 9 And an angel of the Lord suddenly stood before them, and the glory of the Lord flashed and shone around them, and they were terribly frightened. 10 But the angel said to them, "Do not be afraid; for behold, I bring you good news of great joy which will be for [ ] all the people. 11 For this day in the city of David there has been born for you a Savior, who is Christ the Lord (the Messiah). 12 And this will be a sign for you [by which you will recognize Him]: you will find a Baby wrapped in [swaddling] cloths and lying in a manger." 13 Then suddenly there appeared with the angel a multitude of the heavenly host (angelic army) praising God and saying,
14 "Glory to God in the highest [heaven], And on earth peace among men with whom He is well-pleased."

15 When the angels had gone away from them into heaven, the shepherds began saying one to another, "Let us go straight to Bethlehem, and see this [wonderful] thing that has happened which the Lord has made known to us." 16 So they went in a hurry and found their way to Mary and Joseph, and the Baby as He lay in the manger. 17 And when they had seen this, they made known what had been told them about this Child, 18 and all who heard it were astounded and wondered at what the shepherds told them. 19 But Mary treasured all these things, giving careful thought to them and pondering them in her heart. 20 The shepherds returned, glorifying and praising God for all that they had heard and seen, just as it had been told them.

December 26

Be certain that God's Word is true. Wisdom that cannot be learned from the world is contained in the Bible. Let it be your guidebook for the coming new year, and the source of what you sow throughout your days. Don't believe false prophets; they will ruin your crops.

Galatians 6:7

7 Do not be deceived, God is not mocked [He will not allow Himself to be ridiculed, nor treated with contempt nor allow His precepts to be scornfully set aside]; for whatever a man sows, this and this only is what he will reap.

December 27

Living the Christian life can be tiring, and Satan loves to discourage us, sending obstacles and doubts our way. But we have a never-ending power source, God our father, who encourages us and sends showers of mercy and grace to refresh us. Lift your eyes up, and rest in His blessings.

Galatians 6:9

9 Let us not grow weary or become discouraged in doing good, for at the proper time we will reap, is we do not give in.

December 28

It doesn't cost us anything to be gracious. An act of grace on our part can be the turning point in someone's day, or the positive note the spurs another into graciousness on their part. Jesus is the ultimate example of grace in action for us to follow.

Proverbs 22:11

11 He who loves purity of heart and whose speech is gracious will have the king as his friend.

December 29

We sometimes see courage as a big attribute modeled by generals, martyrs, or people such as Mother Teresa. But we need courage in our daily lives to walk as our Lord did, showing His characteristics to those around us. He will freely give you all the courage you need just ask and hold fast to His hand.

Ephesians 5:15-16

15 Therefore see that you walk carefully [living life with honor, purpose, and courage; shunning those who tolerate and enable evil], not as the unwise, but as wise [sensible, intelligent, discerning people], 16 making the very most of your time [on earth, recognizing and taking advantage of each opportunity and using it with wisdom and diligence], because the days are [filled with] evil.

December 30

In all things, God commands we be thankful. This can be hard when we feel our trials are insurmountable. But God uses these times to build our faith, and to mold our character. Thank Him even then.

Isaiah 48:10

10 "Indeed, I have refined you, but not as silver; I have tested and chosen you in the furnace of affliction.

December 31

There is nothing more I wish for you this new year than to find peace and increased faith in your walk with God. Happy New Year in the Lord Jesus Christ!

Isaiah 26:3-4

3 "You will keep in perfect and constant peace the one whose mind is steadfast [that is, committed and focused on You – in both inclination and character], Because he trusts and takes refuge in You [with hope and confident expectation].

4 "Trust [confidently] in the Lord forever [He is your fortress, your shield, your banner],

For the Lord God is an everlasting Rock [the Rock of Ages].

Biography

Jane Joyce retired from the state of Tennessee, and embarked on her second career, that of a Licensed Professional Counselor and director of the William Blevins Institute of Mental Health and Spirituality, Carson-Newman University.

She felt led by the Lord to apply to graduate school for her Master of Counseling when her mother was diagnosed with Alzheimer's and came to live with her and her husband. After the MS was completed, she continued in school and earned an Educational Specialist in Collaboration with Counseling and Education, and an Educational Doctorate in Administrative Leadership.

This book grew out of a four-year ministry on Facebook entitled "I prayed for you today". It is hoped that the daily readings will bring the reader closer to the Lord and inspire them to delve into the Word.

The book is dedicated first and foremost to God, who completed rerouted my life to the riches found in living His plan. Secondly to my husband, Steve, who has encouraged me every step of the way, and believed in me totally. My mentor, Dr. William Blevins, inspired me to attempt that which I never dreamed, and exposed me to the joy of continuing to learn every day.

Special thanks to my graduate assistant, Angela Taylor, who typed her fingers to the bone on this project. Gratitude to Carolyn "Tinker" Amos for her proofreading skills; it took a lot of time, and I really appreciate it.

And of course, Peyton, Sweetness, and Samurai, my furry assistants.

www.ingramcontent.com/pod-product-compliance
Lightning Source LLC
Chambersburg PA
CBHW071913110526
44591CB00011B/1670